# You Can
## Free Yourself
### from the
# KARMA
## of CHAOS

THROUGH

Tina Louise Spalding

# You Can Free Yourself from the KARMA of CHAOS

through Tina Louise Spalding

Light Technology
PUBLISHING

For information about special discounts for bulk purchases,
please contact Light Technology Publishing Special Sales at
1-800-450-0985 or publishing@LightTechnology.net.

ISBN: 978-1-62233-057-7

PO Box 3540
Flagstaff, AZ 86003
1-800-450-0985
1-928-526-1345
www.LightTechnology.com

This book is dedicated to our future selves who
live in a world of peace and harmony. May we all
envision a new society for our children
and ourselves where war is no more; where "Holocaust"
is an unknown word; where everyone receives the
basics of life as a right, not a privilege; and where we
have learned from our past but
never again revisit it.

# Contents

# Preface

It has been almost a year since I started channeling and writing this book, and it has been a busy and an eventful time of personal and professional expansion. My assignment, like yours, seems to be to push the common boundaries of the acceptable and venture into the unknown, unsanctioned, and at times, forbidden worlds that Ananda and their friends introduce us to.

When Ananda told me I would be channeling a book about the Holocaust, I was not particularly happy about it, as you can imagine. At the time, I was housesitting on Salt Spring Island on Canada's west coast during a rainy and cold February. Starting a new project with Ananda (and whoever else might show up to contribute) is a surefire way of brightening up a dark winter, but as soon as I learned the subject matter, my enthusiasm waned considerably. I had the same feelings of trepidation I had when presented with the Jesus material, a feeling that I was entering a forbidden zone. My mind whispered warnings about the dangers of poking this sacred cow, but Ananda assured me all would be well. They told me to take my time — a year, in fact — and to work slowly and steadily through the subject matter and my feelings. My advice to you, the reader, is to do the same.

This book explores our planet's ancient and hidden past as well as the more modern era, and it introduces us to spiritual meanings of some of the events of those periods. It also pushes us to expand our vision of humanity, humanity's connections, and our planet. Ananda, as always, uses gentle words and reassuring prose to take us on these mind-expanding excursions, but be forewarned: This book will definitely challenge you, perhaps unnerve you, and more than likely leave you a bit speechless. It certainly has done all those things to me!

Spiritually, I was raised in a very unconventional way, and I have no doubt that this prepared me from a very early age for many of the unusual experiences I am having as an adult. We had séances in our home when I was a child, and we often visited mediums and psychics. More importantly, we had lots of books that delved into the afterlife, near-death experiences, extraterrestrial contact, and cultures that spent a lot of time in meditation. Although we did not practice anything in particular in our home (other than endless curiosity about these subjects), these books expanded my consciousness to accept that Spirit is living with us and that a lot more is going on than meets the eye. From Edgar Cayce's medical intuition to Lobsang Rampa's Tibetan explorations of consciousness to Ruth Montgomery's channeled texts about life after death, I was well groomed for the work I do now. So when I was asked to channel books, the landscape was somewhat familiar. However, it is very different to experience channeling personally rather than read about it in books. Despite five years of channeling experience and all that early preparation, I was definitely challenged by this book almost as much as I was by *Jesus: My Autobiography* (Light Technology Publishing, 2015).

In alternative media these days, many subjects are arising for contemplation, such as the secret space program, Nazi Germany and its involvement with extraterrestrials, and a planetary history that differs from the one our traditional education gives us. I'm sure many of you have entertained some ideas about the subjects this book explores. But Ananda and the surprise visitors who channel alongside it bring a comprehensive and spiritual take on subjects that are often only approached from a secular and, at times, fearful point of view. This book helps me understand our evolving culture and will help you too, once you get past the shock that some of the content will bring up. Remember, I have been well trained for this job, and perhaps you have not had such wide and varied experiences as I have, so it might upset you to hear some of the words contained in this text. But please do as Ananda suggests: Take it slowly and easily, and allow these new ideas time to expand your consciousness.

If you have read my other books, which Ananda recommends, you have already been prepared for this book and will have less difficulty expanding into this new paradigm. If you have not read my other books, understand that your mind needs information and time to expand from the limiting and fear-inducing beliefs it has been indoctrinated with. Reeducation is required for all of us about our true history and our societal teachings, and this book brings that reeducation to life in spades. Ananda has done everything it can to ease us out of fear and ignorance into truth, and this book continues that challenging journey through our ascension process.

I did not know at the beginning of this project that I would be channeling messages from extraterrestrials as part of it. In fact, had I known, I may well have said no, but as usual, life and my experiences expand me just enough to deal with what Spirit hands out as my next assignment. I have managed to rise above my personal resistance to channeling ET messages for public consumption and have really enjoyed their contributions most of the time. Each ET in this book came through with Ananda's permission because each has humanity's best interests as a mandate. My gatekeepers exert their influence in many realms, it seems, so I trust in the information and the goodness of the speakers' intentions. Ananda has told me that more communications from them are coming my way and to begin a new text totally dedicated to ET communications. There's never a dull moment here! That will be my next project.

I hope you enjoy this book and manage to feel your way through the parts that cause a little tension or upset. You have this book in your hands, so clearly you are ready for your next level of mind-expanding tales from Ananda and the other contributors. You are not reading this book by mistake just as I am not writing this by mistake. We are all on track with our ever-expanding consciousness, bringing into being the frequencies this world needs us to hold in order to usher in a new era of peace and love for all beings on this planet and beyond.

— Tina Louise Spalding

# Introduction

*Ananda*

We are Ananda, and we are a group consciousness. We have dictated many books through this particular channel. She is a dear one to us, and each time we come to her, she is willing to bring forth the messages that we, as a group consciousness, feel are destined for your planet to help you understand the processes of evolution and creation and to help you understand what you are looking at and what you have experienced on your physical plane, this Earth, this three-dimensional reality in which you find yourself.

We have come here to help you because this is a pivotal time in your planet's evolution. You will see monumental changes in your society over the next few years, and to achieve the shifts and changes that these transfigurations are going to bring about, you must come to understand your minds, your histories, and human nature as you experience it on the ground, in your hearts, and in your consciousness.

We are bringing to your conscious awareness information about how you are being and have been manipulated in two subjects: the extraterrestrial contact with your planet and the Holocaust. These two subjects are deeply entwined, and they've contributed to the creation of a society that is fearful, ignorant, and dangerously able to be controlled and directed into war, fear, negativity, and cruelty. All the powers that be on your planet at this time are part of a global conspiracy. This word is regarded very negatively in your society. It has been and still is used to call people foolish or insane or to dismiss many valid arguments, but we use it here because you understand what it means.

A conspiracy consists of a group of people who work to achieve a particular effect using whatever means are at hand to deceive, to cooperate in a large deception. That is what your society is, a demonstration of one of the largest deceptions that has ever taken place. But that deception is coming to an end, and we are part of that deconstruction. We bring to your attention all the means used to get you to participate in this conspiracy in ignorance: your education system, religious systems, cultural prescriptions, money, television, and mass media. All these things are used in this conspiracy to keep you small and frightened and to keep you attacking.

## What to Expect

In this book, we address one of the great horrors of your twentieth century, and that is the killing and torturing of Jewish people by the German Third Reich and Hitler, that horrific journey that the human race went through and continues to go through. It took place many decades ago, but it is a wound that is still unhealed. It is a thought structure that lives in the bodies of many, many beings who have experienced it or have heard about it or who are afraid of it happening again, and it is a very important subject to address.

How can an entire generation be victims or victimize others? This is war, a devastating aspect of ego consciousness that you have experienced and, as we said, continue to experience. It is a subject that has become taboo in your society. You are not allowed to look at it in any other way than the materialistic, physical, egoic way that you have been trained to look at it. It is now time, as you enter this new era of your planet, to understand what truly transpired and the result: What was the cause? What was the result? What happened there?

Even as you read this introduction, you might feel fears arise, and you might feel the social conditioning that you have experienced. You will feel the rules and regulations of your society push against that which we are saying, and we want you to know that it is important for you to feel these discomforts. You have been trained in a belief system that insists you look at this only in one way, and that is why it is being kept alive and why that energy thrives still: You have been forbidden to look at it in any other way than in the sinful way, the judgmental way, the accusing way, and the unforgiving way.

As we venture into this text, we want you to know that you will be shown another version of the story and another way of looking at this kind of devastation. This kind of devastation has happened many times in your society. There have been massacres and mass extinctions and social atrocities throughout your history, but this one continues to live in the hearts and minds of many. We must address it so that you can move into the new world — your new elevating and increasing frequency of consciousness — without old baggage. This baggage, the judgments, and the fears must be released. You must enter this new world, this new time on your planet, with clear and uncontaminated minds. It is our purpose to bring you through this journey so that you can understand, forgive, and walk unencumbered into your new future.

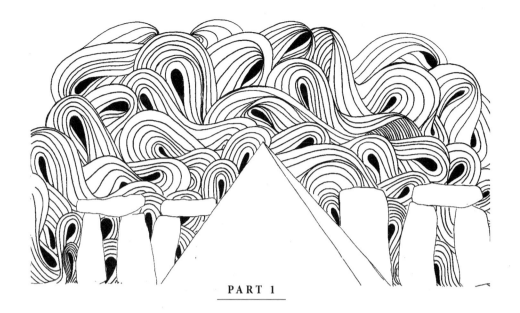

PART 1

# A History Misunderstood

*Ananda*

# CHAPTER 1

# You Are
# Being Manipulated

Your society is collapsing, and we make no bones about it. We are not here to keep you comfortable. We are not here to tell you what you want to hear, because that is what has been happening. We are here to tell you the truth, and the truth is that you are being led inexorably toward a precipice of disaster.

"How is this happening, and who is doing it?" you ask. Well, you have been led astray in your society, and we are about to tell you a story that will be very difficult for you to hear. It will be disturbing because it will make you question everything. It will make you question every thing you hold to be true about reality, and in that questioning, you will become angry with us. You will become frustrated with us because it will seem that what we are telling you cannot be true. We want you to know a great deception has been played on your society not only in the past few years (although it has escalated) but also over millennia.

You have been led like sheep to the slaughter through lies and deceit so that hierarchies of many origins can reap the wealth and benefits of your hard labor and your energy systems. Yes, your energy systems are being harvested for fuel by these hierarchies. Through manipulations of your mind and technology, they harvest the energy of your fear. This fear is generated intentionally in your minds, and it is taught to you from birth. It has been taught to your parents and their parents and their parents' parents, so you cannot see it. You are swimming in these lies, your parents have been swimming in these lies, and generation after generation has been swimming in these lies. Thus, they have become invisible. They have become the very matrix of your experience, so it seems as if they are true, and it seems as if they must always be that way.

This deception has been systematic, and it has been very well orchestrated by very intelligent beings. This is the difficulty you face. You are very, very intelligent beings, but you have been dumbed down. You have been taught to eat foods that dumb you down. You have been taught to read materials that dumb you down. Most of all, you have been trained to be entertained by frequencies of a very low dimension that have a detrimental effect on your health, your well-being, and your society's ability to survive.

"What has this to do with the Holocaust?" you ask. Well, it is one of those great fearmongering exercises that the hierarchies orchestrated so that you would become terrified, and what a good job they did! You are still afraid to look at this subject, decades after its cessation. This is the kind of act that has been perpetrated to inflict the terror in the collective consciousness that is required for these beings of negative frequency and negative ambition to thrive. They thrive off your inability to see the truth, and they thrive off your inability to realize your personal power.

## You Are Holy Beings

Those of you who have read the books we have written so far through this being know that we are all about you finding your connection to the Divine. We are all about you finding your truth, your self-expression, and your ability to manifest whatever you wish because day by day you manifest everything that you wish even though you do not realize it. However, you have been taught to wish for the wrong things. You have been taught to worry about things, you have been taught to fear things, and you have been indoctrinated in consuming goods and accumulating possessions. This keeps you very fearful because in your training, you are told that the more things you have, the more valuable you are and the more power you wield. In fact, the opposite is true. Those of you who own a lot of things become fearful of losing them rather than joyful in using them.

This is the programming you have been through, and we have touched on many of these things in some of the books we have written.

Now we will go into the darkest parts of this truth. We will now go into the depths of your society and the dark underbelly of the creatures and beings manipulating your psychology, your economy, and your energy systems for a very long time. So we must go far back in the history of your planet. We must go way back in time, before you even knew time existed. We must go back to before your planet began to tell you this story so that you can understand it, so that you will be able to believe it, and so that you will be able to eventually change your minds.

We are not here to terrify you. Your society has done a very good job of that. We are here to remove the fears, anxieties, and the misunderstandings from your minds. We are here to align you with the reality of what has happened on your planet, and we are here to align you with the truth of your magnificence and your holiness.

Yes, you are holy beings. You are made of love, from love, and for love, yet you have been transformed into beings that are hateful, fearful, judgmental, and warring, and it is time that you understand the history of your world, the history of your planet, the history of your revolutions, and the history of your murderous and devastating catastrophes.

Your world has been a playground for darkness for a long time, but light is coming your way. There are millions of us who are nonphysical. We are extraterrestrial in the sense that we do not live on your planet, but not in the way that you think of extraterrestrials. We are highly evolved consciousnesses that have come here to help you climb out of the pit of terror that has assaulted your minds and trained your hearts and souls for so long now. It is a long journey out of that pit, and you have gone deep into the caverns of fear and darkness. We have to hold up a light and tell you to trust us. We ask you to trust us to tell you the truth.

We want you to know that the truth will feel good. The lies that you have been fed do not feel good, and they do not create good things. You must look around to see what is happening on your planet. You must see the slave trade of young children and girls for sexual purposes. You must see the industry of pornography and lust that is secretly driving your young people insane. You must see the devastation of the drugs and alcohol used to mask the true feelings of your souls, and you must see the rape and pillaging of your planet as her beautiful resources and energies are taken from her very heart and soul.

Our job is to bring the truth to you, as hard as it is, so that you can reconfigure your minds and your hearts to use your influence and creative power with your brothers and sisters for good. But until you know the truth, until you know what has been done to you, you will not be able to do this. So we must take you into your planet's past. We must take you into your planet's history so that you understand where this dark seed was planted and how you can uproot it from deep within your minds and hearts so that it will not grow again.

# CHAPTER 2

# Earth's Long History

The history that you have been deceptively fed through your education system is a mere microcosm of the magnificent and very, very long history that intelligent life has had on your planet. Billions of years ago, before your planet was even really formed, there were very evolved societies throughout the universe. This is not a story you have been told, but you are starting to hear snippets of it now. We want to bring forth these ideas because a revolution of exposition is happening on your planet. You will be shown everything that has been hidden from you, so it is important that you have the story from an accurate source. That is why we are here.

We have been informed of the disclosure that will transpire on your planet, the stories that will be revealed, and it is important for you to have the documentation to go through this exposition, this unfolding, with guidance because without it, your minds will not survive. These books are that guidance. They are designed, book by book and layer by layer, to reveal thoughts and concepts that must be integrated into the mind for you to go through this transition in a sane and (we would say) "civilized" way; however, that word has been very poorly used on your planet.

## Many Civilizations Came Before

Billions of years ago intelligent life thrived and grew. The consciousness that is the Divine, what you call God, has been inserting itself into physical form to gather experience for a very, very long time. This play of separation and duality has been going on for a very, very long time. It did not start 5,000, 6,000, or even 10,000 years ago, as you have been instructed. These are pernicious lies told to keep your focus very limited and fearful, let us say. If you had known about the history of your world and your universe and if you had understood that there were thousands of civilizations of much more highly evolved states than your own, then you would not have believed the stories you were fed from your religious teachers about God creating you and his one beloved son that you have so fervently believed in. We are pulling the rug out from under this.

We have been building a wonderful foundation for this revelation. Now you must understand, as you go into this book, that several books precede this, and as a recommendation for the stability of your mind, we suggest you read those books first because there are ideas and energies that are intimated in those words that will help you integrate this information. So if this is the first book of ours that you have read, we ask you to stop right now and read the other ones so that you can build the energies toward this unfolding, toward this opening of your collective consciousness.

Your collective consciousness has been built over millennia by the structures and hierarchies that have ruled your planet. The very nature of your psyche is dependent on the stories those hierarchies have told you, and you will witness (and may even be witnessing at this time) people on your planet not doing very well once these revelations come into minds that are unprepared. It is very much like running a marathon after you have done nothing but sit on a couch: You will not make it, and you will injure yourself severely. This is likely to happen in your society as these truths are revealed.

Technologically advanced societies observed your planet as it developed and evolved. As it came into being, additions were made. Your Moon was added as a stabilizing factor and as a place to store magnetic, balancing information. You witness this in your tides that respond to the Moon. That was one of the jobs it was assigned, as was being a place for these galactic explorers to store supplies and operate from. They knew that as your planet developed, they would infuse it with life and genetic material, and as it came to that part of its evolution, they would implant and disseminate and distribute different forms of life there. They knew they would engineer certain kinds of physical structures to see what they could do and how they learned. Your human race was one of these implantations, we would say.

Your story about Adam and Eve was a poorly remembered and inaccurate concept that traveled from the distant past of your planet, and that implementation of genetic and consciousness experience was not the first. It is the most recent recollection you have in your society, so it has survived, but eons ago other beings were introduced. Other populations were integrated into that surface population, and you have layer over layer of genetic experimentation, development, and understanding playing out on your planet's surface.

Now, there have been great geological shifts on your planet as well, tremendous and tumultuous catastrophes, we would say. If you lived near them at the time, they ruined your civilization, but there have been a lot of extracurricular activities (we are going to use that phrase because it means that they were not planned or part of the design). As you have evolved on your planet, there have been many fractures and iterations and separations of your races through various events — some of them wars, some of them natural disasters, and some of them natural evolution. And throughout this history, visitors from other planets have come to your society. They have presented themselves as gods to give you information and designs to assist in your evolution, and they have come in the form of demons to torment and scare you. This is a long part of your history that has been hidden from your view in an attempt to keep you very shortsighted and conceited. When you believe you are the only beings in the universe, you can become arrogant and unloving, and as we have said, being unloving is something some of these extraterrestrial beings have wanted from you.

You have heard about ancient civilizations, such as Atlantis and Lemuria, and these are hidden in the depths of your planet's history, its transfigurations and its transformations. These real places were not necessarily accurately described in your mythologies, but they were great civilizations that lived and thrived on your planet millennia ago. The timelines are irrelevant at this point. We do not want you to get caught up in when this happened and get stuck in the past; we are merely telling you the histories so that you can understand the length and depth and breadth of your interaction, as a planet, with extraterrestrial beings. This is the most important thing for you to understand in this chapter. Yes, this is all leading up to the Holocaust, so do not dismiss this as an unwarranted tangent. It is warranted. We are explaining how you came to be, which is very important because it is how you allowed this atrocity to occur.

## Free Will and Duality

In your planet's evolution, you have been in a constant state of duality. Now we will explain that a little bit here. You have come down into physical, material separation from love, from oneness, and you have entered into that place of "lack of love." You see this in your world at this time, this lack of love: the warring nature, the judgments, the isolation, and the separation that people, countries, and even continents experience. This happened in your past as well, and on your planet, you have had the play of dark and light going on throughout its history. You have had the play of the oppressor, and you have had the play of the oppressed. You have had the play of the manipulator, and you have had the play of the manipulated throughout your history, and that is why even in your short history, you have seen endless disasters and plagues and conflagrations and holocausts.

You can see the repetitious pattern of power wielding cruelty and murder and judgment over those who have been designated as the victims. The victors and the victims — that is the endless play of life that has been going on, on your planet for a very long time. It was allowed to continue because of free choice. The beings who manifested in physical structures, regardless of their form, were given the free will to choose that expression. They were given the free will to experience that demonstration and evolution that took place. Yes, entire civilizations have come and gone, but once you understand that you are not a body, once you understand that consciousness infuses itself into many different forms, then you begin to understand that the ebb and flow of life on your planet is not as negative as you think it is. And that is where we take you in the next chapter — into the principles of evolution and what you call reincarnation and karma — so that you can begin to understand what has transpired and is still transpiring on your planet.

The limited, materialistic, "one life" view causes the suffering you experience. Once you understand the great and eternal nature of your consciousness and the great and eternal nature of your being and its exploration of itself, then you will see the life-and-death dramas that play out on your planet as much less cruel, much less devastating, and more easily understood.

# CHAPTER 3

# The Universe Is Your Mirror

As you experience your current life, you have, through your indoctrination, become deeply entrenched in the physical and material world. This is a consequence of your consumer programming, and this has been going on for several generations as your mass media expands, increasing its effect and its constant delivery of messages. These messages are designed to keep you in the physical/material world and fearful. So when you look at the world through this lens of distortion, it is hard to accept death, suffering, and oppression because you do not see past the nose on your face. You have been brought into a tremendously shortsighted view of reality. This is not how it is.

You must remember that you can believe things that are untrue, and when you, as a society, have been told things that are not true, your culture becomes profoundly separated from what is actually happening. That is the situation you in the Western world find yourselves in. Minds have been shut down, brought incrementally and intentionally lower and lower in frequency, and now it's as if you are crawling on your hands and knees, unable to see above the grass through which you are moving to the landscape beyond. It looks as if there is only grass — the physical/material world — and your bodies, and they become all that you understand exists. There are many beautiful landscapes and experiences that you are not having because of this limited worldview.

## Recognize Your Frequency

How does this relate to reincarnation and karma, subjects that are liberally thrown around now in your society? Well, karma is the belief that there is some retribution happening: If you perpetrate a crime against somebody, you will fall victim to that same crime (or something similar), or some kind of accident will befall you. There is some intention behind it, some retribution underlying the action. Karma does not play out that way. All the universe does is interpret frequency, and there are many frequencies. There are many experiences, people, places, and things within each frequency realm.

When you reside in a high-frequency realm, you experience things such as love, peace, equanimity, creativity, freedom, and these kinds of things. If you are in a lower-frequency realm, you experience sickness, poverty, shame, worry, and these kinds of things. In that realm, you meet other people of a similar frequency. Now, when you are in that frequency and emitting that frequency, you continue to experience people, places, and things of that frequency. So when you are shame based and defensive, let us say, you will encounter things of a like frequency. When you are shame based and defensive, you might be harsh in the way you act with other people because you want to keep yourself protected. Perhaps you are a little aggressive as well. These are some of the variations and permutations of that frequency, and there are endless permutations and generations of it (generations in the sense of making things happen). As long as you stay in that frequency, you will appear to receive negative experiences when you act in a less than loving way.

This is where most of you reside. Most of you have a social face, and the outside looks a lot higher in frequency than it actually is. Remember, it is not your smiling face that generates this; it is your thoughts and the energy and intention behind those thoughts. You might put on nice clothes and a happy face and go to work looking as if you are civilized and nice, but in your heart, you might be judging yourself as ugly or fat or unsuccessful and judging others as perhaps the same thing. Generally, it is not that varied. So the lower frequency within the heart and mind generates your experience, and this is why karma is so confusing for you. You are all well behaved on the outside, and you pretend to be nice a lot of the time, but inside, a very different frequency is being emitted.

You see what seem to be very calm and civilized lives riddled with accidents and disease and seemingly random negative events. Of course, they are not random at all; they are being generated from within those hearts and minds, and it becomes difficult to understand because you have been trained to be superficial. You have been trained by listening to your inner self, and there is a great contrast between the face you present to the world and your inner face, your inner consciousness. This is why you sometimes say, "Bad things happen to good people." These are some of the mythologies that you have created in your society to try to explain what you think of as very difficult, seemingly random, and arbitrary dispensations of negativity. You think it is from past lives, but generally it is from the true frequency that you hold.

## The Opportunities of Reincarnation

You live in a reflective universe that brings your frequency into physical manifestation in the form of people, places, things, and events to show you what your true frequency is. This is a great gift from the universe. It shows you exactly where your frequency is in a completely nonjudgmental way. It does not say you are good or bad; it says you are "this" frequency — that is all. You might choose to stay there, or you might choose to lower or raise your frequency. There is no moral judgment. There is no God saying that "this" should be so or not so. This is a freewill zone. You are allowed to do whatever you wish, and you have come here to do whatever you wish.

Now, in reincarnation terms, the same thing is happening, but over a longer timeline. If you are living a life that is happy and joyful and creative and self-expressive, you will raise your frequency throughout that incarnation, and you will experience in your next iteration, which we call a lifetime, a higher frequency.

For example, you are born into a certain frequency. Perhaps your family is a little rough around the edges and not very good at loving you. It reflects your frequency as you were born. That came with this particular incarnation's frequency plan, we will say. You were born into that family for a reason. It suited your frequency. But as you traveled through your life, you learned a lot of things. You studied spiritual material to understand the truth of creation. You focused your mind, you learned to forgive your family for their harsh ways, and you became gentler. You developed your connection to Spirit and to your own creativity, and as you passed on from that particular incarnation, your frequency was higher than when you started. Even though you look at babies as innocents, they are already holding a frequency from their previous or other incarnations. This is how it goes.

The opposite, of course, would be true as well, if you were born into a family of a particular frequency and you continued to model that frequency. Perhaps they were a little rough around the edges, and you continued that family trait. Perhaps they stole a little here and there, deceived others, drank, and fought. You fit into that mold very well because, of course, it was your frequency, and as you drank more and fought more, you became more angry and closed off and aggressive. As you traveled through that incarnation, you lowered your frequency, and perhaps you even died an unfortunate death because of the frequency you held. Based on that experience, your next incarnation would be less than ideal. You would come into a family of a lower frequency again. This is happening over and over because that is all that this place is.

### Teachings Come in a Variety of Packages

This place is a reflective universe. It always has been a reflective universe, and it always will be a reflective universe. That is why it is so important for these teachings to be understood. The rules do not change, and that is why you see golden threads between different religions. Information was brought in a revelatory state or through contact with Spirit or higher consciousness to particular beings. These universal truths were transmitted, and then the ego mind — the religious aspect — took over, and structures were built around particular sacred experiences or dissemination of information. Human minds then began to make up other rules and regulations about how to play out this game of life. That is what you see in all your religions.

Each original contact had a thread of truth given to him or her either in a short period or over a lifetime, and in that experience, the person encountered higher-frequency teachings from beings of higher mind. But in that lifetime, he or she encountered the ego mind and lower consciousness, and the creative, earthbound thoughts and beliefs of human nature came into play. Then religions were built around that person's expressions.

# CHAPTER 4

# You Are Not
# Your True Selves

The systems that are working on your minds at this time, as we have said many times, have been long in the making. We are using your history to show you where these structures come from. Unless you know where they came from, you cannot treat them with the correct attitude and understand how pervasive your society's conditioning has been. You will believe the newscasts, the rumors, and the traditions of your society, and you will continue to be indoctrinated. We are here to bring you out of that indoctrination and to show you who you truly are. We are not here to upset you for no reason; we are here to bring the truth. Unfortunately, because the truth has been hidden from you and you have been lied to, you will become upset. You must understand that as difficult as this is to hear, the information we are bringing through is important.

We have told you that there were many civilizations from other planetary systems who came to see you and who, in fact, engineered you and continue to do so. This is something that is a little distressing for you. Because of your religious histories, you think you have naturally evolved over a very short time. That is not so. Your planet was seeded with life many times and has been interfered with many times. The original seeding was high frequency in its intention to bring a very rich and varied genetic library, we would say, to your Earth plane.

This is where your flora and fauna were originally developed. They did not naturally evolve from microorganisms into these other things; they were genetically engineered. Some of them were created in the likeness of their creators, and that is where the stories of lizard and reptilian masters arose. It is indeed true that genetic experiments taking place on your planet were led by these beings. Many of the dinosaurs were reptilians of high intelligence. You have made judgments about the intelligence and the abilities of reptiles. You have decided that they were small-brained and inefficient creatures, but this was not so.

The genetic experiments that took place at that time were done by highly intelligent reptilian species who replicated their genetics and placed it on the planet in the form of these giant creatures. Their extinctions had many different causes. Some you have right, and some you have wrong, but these are not issues we want to belabor at this point. We are merely telling you that you have had influences on your society that are not simple, are not always in your best interests, and are not always humanoid, so you see your history incorrectly.

## You Can Reduce Your Suffering

You have been part of a grand experiment. You had many levels of awareness coming into this experiment, and some of them were much higher than others. We are high up in that caring, loving, benevolent realm situated in unity consciousness and love. Many of the extraterrestrial encounters you have had were in the lower realms of your level of consciousness and even beneath that. These are some of the causes of the trials and tribulations on your planet. Because you have been kept ignorant of your beautiful, loving nature and trained to be aggressive, judgmental consumers, you are ignorant of your natural selves, and that is why you suffer on your plane at this time.

You suffer because within your energetic system and your consciousness, you are meant to function at a much higher level than you are. Because of teachings and the long training program you have been in, you have forgotten where you come from and what you are. The suffering you experience signals that you are not in accord with yourself. You think you suffer because the world is a bad place and people are bad and there is no joy to be had, but the truth is that you suffer because you are not your true selves. You are not the unaltered souls you are destined to be.

The complex and elaborate nature of your evolution is too much to go into in this book. It would take volume after volume to tell you what has transpired on your planet, and other beings are doing that. Other beings have been assigned the task to bring into print the history of your planet. We are merely mentioning its complex and convoluted nature so that you open your minds to the idea that things are not as they seem.

Next, we go into a more complex discussion of reincarnation so that you understand the spiritual journey you are on as a collective. This is very different from the individual journeys you are on within duality. A higher form of consciousness is directing you. A higher form of consciousness is orchestrating how you grow and learn, and you must go through the process of physical incarnation to actually integrate the lessons in your consciousness. As you understand the principles of reincarnation and physical incarnation, you will see how some of these seeming disasters transpire.

We have laid some simple foundations for you, and now we will go into this subject a little more deeply so that you have a true and complete comprehension of incarnation, reincarnation, the physical, and the spiritual, all of which are playing out on your planet. There have been many civilizations, interventions, and interferences made in your development. It is not a simple, short line as you have been told.

# CHAPTER 5

# The Glorious Exploration of Consciousness

Your society is deeply indoctrinated in believing in the physical, and this has not been accidental. Keeping you occupied with the physical prevents you from tapping into your power. It prevents you from tapping into your godlike quality we have referred to so many times throughout our teachings. This has been intentional so that the powers that be who understand the laws of creation and the power of your individual consciousnesses can use it for their purposes. As you come to understand creation, free will, and your connection to the Divine, you will feel that penny drop in your mind: Something has been afoot in your culture, and it is not in your best interests.

We will build this concept slowly so that it does not jar you too much and you are not so offended that you walk away from this material. That does not serve us. We must open your mind, little by little, and allow you to contemplate and integrate and sit with these ideas because the mind is a structure. Do not feel that we are pussyfooting around or prevaricating about this subject. We are not. We are dealing with a structure that is built, one idea at a time, and that is your belief system.

In the Western world, you have fundamental beliefs that are untrue and that support the other beliefs you act on every minute of every day. So you must understand that this deconstruction — or reconstruction — process must be very lovingly approached. If we go into your minds and dismantle foundational beliefs by removing them and challenging them, your psychology will become upset and out of balance in such a way that it might fall or fail, which you would consider an anxiety attack or a psychotic episode. You might even shut the information down because it causes your mind too much disruption.

## The Mind Seeks Peace

Remember, the mind always wants to be peaceful. That is where it functions best. If you are full of untrue ideas and beliefs that are in conflict with the truth that we introduce, you will feel anxious, and the mind will try to return to a place of balance and equanimity. It might use drugs and alcohol or food to do that, and it will delete or refuse to entertain information that causes too much upset. So know that if you feel what we call a little "tippy" — you feel unsure or begin to feel a little anxious — just take a break from the information, and allow yourself to integrate the beliefs and concepts that we have introduced. Then come back a few days later after you have calmed down and contemplated these ideas and have somewhere to put them in your consciousness.

If some of you are completely unable to integrate this material in your mind, and if you find this book does that to you because the ideas are too new or too radical, go back to our earlier texts *Making Love to God* and *Great Minds Speak to You*. These are introductory texts to some of these concepts, and they hold an introductory frequency, in that sense. You will be holding texts that are laden with information in energetic form, and they will gently shift your worldview and your self-concept. They will assist you in building a wonderful new structure that will be a free mind. This is what we are trying to get you to — a mind that is free of indoctrination and listens to the inner guidance Spirit has given to you as a gift on your journey.

We remind you that your feeling/emotional self is your connection to Spirit, your connection to divine information, and the peace in your mind is the quality in which that information flows most freely. So the lessons in *A Course in Miracles* and these books are designed to relieve your mind from stress and to bring you back to a place of quiet and peaceful presence. In that state, you can listen to your guidance system more accurately and clearly. But for you to do that, of course, we must teach you the truth of your reality and your personal experience. This information teaches what reincarnation really is and how it functions so that you can apply these truthful principles to your life and allow them to affect your behavior. Remember, your behavior comes from what you think, and thinking comes from what you believe is true. As we introduce new ideas to you, they will facilitate a change in your behavior that perhaps has been difficult for you to accomplish with the belief structure you hold at this time that is contaminated with untrue ideas.

### Spiritual Repression Is Easing

The idea of death is one of your great fears. Reincarnation shifts your consciousness on this idea. The reincarnation you have been taught is considerably contaminated by your beliefs in the body and time. All who live in a body in this third-dimensional reality you call life have tangible, physical experiences that you believe prove death and time are real and that this is the only place you will ever be. This is a function of the focused mind that is required to experience physical reality, but it is not true in and of itself. It is an aspect of a limited experience to bring you into intense focus so that you can have the experience.

If you knew what you truly were — if you had all the information streaming into your conscious mind about your past, concurrent, and future lives — you would be completely overwhelmed, and you would not be able to function at all. This information is filtered out for good reason: so that you can sit and write a poem, make love to your partner, or sit on a log to contemplate a sunset. These are experiences that are very valuable in your consciousness evolution, and were you to be inundated with every piece of information that your higher self has access to, you would be overcome.

You see this in some of the beings you consider to be psychotic. They are tapping into other realities and realms, and because you have such prohibitions on this kind of talent, you put these people in institutions and medicate them into silence so that you do not have to hear what they tell you. Some of the beings who stand on the roadside with signs and some who seem to be insane are actually tapping into these realities. If your society were more in tune with truth, it would assist those beings in coping with what are, at times, considerable gifts to bring that information through in a more controlled way (through training and so on).

When it comes to spiritual information, you have a completely repressed society, but we are very happy to say it is slowly opening, and we are doing our best to open the minds of millions of people through these teachings with Jesus and other beings. Channeling is one way we access closed minds because the more open ones among you will allow channeling to happen, and the information can come through. Books are less threatening than seeing somebody channel or commune with other spirits in person. These are challenging things for the completely closed and repressed mind, which much of your society has in relation to these communications.

So you have had restricted access, let us say. Those who have the capability are given more access, and that is what you see in this being. In her self-training program and with guidance from us, she has learned how to do this work. She is an intermediary between other dimensions and realms and her own. Not everybody is willing and able to do this particular service for humanity so that you may come to understand your own experiences better. You are not receiving truthful information from your teachers and your religions. You are not getting truthful information from your parents because they too have been indoctrinated in a system of lies and deception that have been manipulating you for millennia.

## There's More to You than You Know

In terms of incarnation, you are not a physical being; you are consciousness housed in a physical structure. Your body is nothing in and of itself. It is nothing without the consciousness that inhabits it, that motivates it, that drives it, that teaches it, and that uses it as an experiential intermediary. You use your body to feel, interpret, and (unfortunately) project. This is a downside, but we will go into projection and how it confuses you later.

In an ideal world, you would be raised in a loving family that would pay attention to what you enjoy and don't enjoy and would shepherd you along your path of evolution with very attentive and caring concern. If you lived in such a society (which there will be at some point on your planet — sooner than you think, in fact), your guidance system, your feeling self, would have spoken very early about things it was interested in. It would have had contact with past incarnations that your parents would have made notes about and perhaps would have even had contact with if they had been that evolved. If they weren't, they would listen to your stories about past incarnations, and they would use those to learn how to treat you.

For example, if you were wealthy in a past life and had memories of owning very expensive things and of being very well treated and then you came into your next incarnation with very expensive taste, the ignorant parent might judge you and say, "Well, you cannot have nice things because we don't have the money for them." An informed parent who had heard your stories of incarnation as a wealthy person, perhaps a royal being, would have much more compassion and understanding for you and might have even bought you the occasional nice thing so that you would not be distressed by not having them. It would bring a completely different taste and quality to your next incarnation.

These are some of the things that happen in your society. Children have memories of other societies and cultures and refer to them as home, and their descriptions are shut down and dismissed as fairy tales and fantasies. The children might even be chastised for lying or telling untruths. This dumbs you down and prevents you from tapping into a wonderful panorama and complex library of information that is available when you train your mind and understand the structure of your incarnational history.

## The Reality About Time and Space

Envision a three-dimensional grid with thousands of vertical and horizontal intersecting lines, and each intersection is a lifetime. Each intersection is connected to every other lifetime through that web of connecting lines. These are thoughts, imaginations, and dreams that you all experience in this particular incarnation. Some of your dreams are from other lifetimes, some of your inspirations are from other lifetimes, and some of your passions are from other lifetimes, and they are all interconnected, offering an endless supply of energy. In some circumstances, such as when you shut down your creativity or dismiss your dreaming life, you are, in fact, dismissing the opportunity for great education and growth. Another life is having another experience in another time and place, and it is gaining some understanding and lessons from that experience and downloading it into the entire system. This would be considered your oversoul, or higher self — the system of all these incarnations — exploring, growing, learning, and sharing information.

When you look at your body as one of those intersections and your personality as one aspect of this greater oversoul, this higher self, then you begin to realize that some of the things you believe do not make sense. Some of the things you believe about life and death do not make sense because you do not possess one body and one life; you are the participant in a glorious exploration of consciousness by higher mind. That is what is happening.

Each aspect of higher mind has thousands of intersecting incarnations, interchangeable information, and so on and so forth. It is a fractal consciousness experience. And as you go up from your consciousness into higher realms, there is a similar setup. In a collective such as ours, you encounter an aware oversoul that has conscious access to all lifetimes, all experiences, and all dimensions and timelines. That is why we have access to so much information. Obviously, you have access to that information as well when you are trained and educated properly. We encourage you to go through this process.

You are one of those many intersections collecting and sharing information. Some of those other incarnations will receive information from you in the form of ideas or inspirations. Somebody from the past might have an idea of a future lifestyle with strange devices that connect you to each other. If the being in that incarnation shares that information (after having a dream or an inspiration of it), his or her friends who are not tuned in that way might say, "That is impossible. You are crazy."

This happens throughout time and space in all convolutions and dimensions and realities. There is not one timeline along which your lifetimes take place. That is an illusion. In this time and place, you have been so focused on the material and forced to believe and value only the physical that it has become your only reality. Other times and places are not deeply indoctrinated in the material, so youngsters come in with flexible and fluid minds that can tap into other timelines. There are, indeed, other beings on your current timeline, in your current time and space, who can dip into other dimensions, commune with other beings, shift other energies in other times and places, and do healing work throughout these realities. These being might be considered shamans in your society, and many are incredible channels and psychics who work very quietly behind the scenes. You might not even notice them. Because they live such an interesting life inside their minds and hearts, they do not need to spend much time out in the physical world.

You are often deceived that the flamboyant teacher knows the most. That is not so. Most brilliant spiritual teachers are very quiet in their demeanor and studies. It is time now for those of you who have been ignorant and indoctrinated to have the truth.

This information is beneficial to you, so pay attention to it. Reread this chapter, and think about some of the ideas, imaginings, dreams, and inspirations that you have ignored. Pay more attention to them. They are educational, they are enlightening, and they are going to help you expand your mind so that you can deal much more easily with the changes and transformations that are coming.

# CHAPTER 6

# The Systemic Reducers of Frequency

The integrity of the mind is at play in your world, and this is why we speak about this particular subject. When a subject causes fear or disturbance in the mind, the mind is not aligned with truth. That is how you know a subject has been contaminated with untruth: It makes you feel bad, or you react with fear. Those of you who are cautiously exploring this book are brave indeed. You are on the leading edge of thinking in your society. You have picked this book up because you are curious about the spiritual meaning of the Holocaust.

There have been many holocausts, of course, but this one has been spotlighted and manipulated by the modern media. There has been a great manipulation of the collective consciousness of your planet since the early 1940s. This is when some serious interventions were made, and the collective mind was seen as a resource, something that could be used and manipulated into certain frequencies to achieve certain ends, and so this is what has been happening on your planet.

Now, we want you to think about this a little bit. Think back to the post-war-era 1940s and the increase in technology and the increase in abundance on your planet. Single-family dwellings became popular, and the modern machinery of the nuclear family — refrigerators and stoves and televisions — came into the home. These are some of the systems used to entice the mind into complacency, and that has happened over these past generations. You have, increment by increment, been led down a path of increasing comfort, and in that comfort, you have become complacent. You have become willing to ignore injustice, and you have become willing to ignore pain and suffering in other parts of the world so long as your comfort is not affected in any way. This has been done intentionally.

You have been indoctrinated in a world of violence through television. It began with shows about cultures taking over other cultures — the battles between the good guy and the bad guy, cowboys and Indians, and gangsters and lawmen. These were the initial manipulative devices used to make violence palatable for you. The "good guy" was always "forced" into violence. He had no other choice. This was deeply indoctrinated in your society. As you evolved through the decades into the 1960s and 1970s, you were taught that violence was the solution, the way. This, of course, has paved the road for increased violence not only on your television screens but also in your world. You have become generations raised on violence. It was not brought in all at one time; it was incrementally brought in with a profound understanding of the consciousness and frequency of the ego mind and the results that would be created from this kind of manipulation.

You see an increase in sicknesses and obesity, and this is a direct result of the extreme attachment to comfort and self-comforting foods that you have been trained to want by, once again, your social and mass media. You have been groomed, if you will, into a place where you will tolerate all kinds of violence in the name of righteousness, the name of good, and the name of capitalism. You have been indoctrinated in the religion of capitalism. These forces are at play from hierarchies that are amassing great amounts of wealth and power and influence through these processes.

## The Fight Isn't Over Oil

You are seeing the financial system filter the money out of your society. You all agree that your money does not buy as much as it used to and that you have to work harder for less. This is not your imagination. The funds from your society are being filtered up through levels of banking and economic manipulation into the hands of the very few, and those hands are wealthy indeed. They have created a powerful and well-orchestrated system of psychological manipulation.

Why are we telling you this in a book about the Holocaust? Well, the mass murder that took place — and was indeed a horrific thing for the world to witness — has been used as one of the implements of manipulation. This is going to be very controversial. The continued marketing of this particular atrocity (through mass media, war movies, and television programs that document over and over again this brutal regime) has led you to extreme judgment and separation and, therefore, a low frequency. It is one of the tools that was used to reduce your frequency in the 1950s and 1960s. This continues in the Middle East, and the wars and violence taking place there arise from the defense of certain structures and countries that count on the fearmongering that has gone on for several decades. They are counting on the fearmongering to continue to propagate and justify increasing violence and militarism.

These decades of indoctrination have been building into a system of finance, a system of thermonuclear development, and a system of industrialization and militarism that has focused its attention on the Middle East. The attention on the Middle East is interesting. Many of you believe it is based on oil, and that is part of it, the human part of it — the material part of it, we will say — but there is another part, the energetic part. That is truly what is at play in the Middle East.

There are vortexes and access points into other dimensions and traversing points, we will say — for example, time-travel portals — located in that part of the world that are very, very precious and are being used by higher-ranking beings on your planet. They travel in and out of this area to other dimensions and galaxies, and they use the material of the area as a means to explain why they are doing what they are doing. That material is the oil. You must understand that there are greater forces than simple economic ones. Galactic forces are involved, and the vortexes and the access points that are being fought over are very valuable because they allow traversing different times and space. This allows great influence to be wielded on your planet, and this influence causes much of the suffering you experience.

Incredible manipulations are taking place (out of sight) culturally and economically and financially, and they are bringing forth the lower frequencies required to maintain control over populations. Understand that the frequency of your planet has been directly manipulated through the repetition of a history that is inaccurately portrayed.

Now, the Holocaust did happen. Many, many beings were killed through the feeding and nurturing of hatred, judgment, and separation mentality. We are not saying that did not happen, but it has been used to perpetuate this energy. The story has been used to manipulate you and control and manipulate the Middle East region of your planet. All kinds of atrocities and military interventions can be justified, and all kinds of crises can be explained away.

Many beings are part of this warlordism, and they are having a very good time of it because none of you are aware of what is actually going on. You have been trained to allow these kinds of interventions through violent shows and your history education that trains you to believe that because the Holocaust happened, anything is allowed and can be justified. That is why you have allowed Israel to be as violent and militaristic and aggressive as it has been.

Things are not as they seem in the Middle East, and we continue this story over the next few chapters so that you understand what is happening on your planet and that it is important for you to raise your frequency. This is what it always comes down to, dear ones. It is important to understand what has been done to your minds, your beliefs, and your frequency level so that you can shift back up into the higher realms where love, peace, prosperity, and communion lie. As long as you are willing to be manipulated and to stay comfortable and in fear, you will contribute to the loss of balance and health and love on this planet. This is what the hierarchies are counting on. It is what they are working to maintain, and it is what we are here to help dispel.

We are pleased to be with you on this journey toward raising your frequency, but to do that, we must open all the doors and cupboards that have been closed, and we must bring forth information that is going to allow you to completely understand why raising your frequency is so important at this time.

We are here to help your planet. We have been sent, and we have been called. You called us with your plea for a better world. You called us with the pleas to help save your planet. You are all inadvertently participating in the lowering of your frequency and the frequency of those beings you share this planet with. We are here to help you understand what has brought you to this place. It has not been intentional on each person's part, but you must all come to see the part you play. As teachers, as highly evolved beings, and as bringers of the light and a new dawning age, we must bring the truth to you, as difficult as it is for you to hear. You must begin to shift your frequency, disconnect yourself from those systems that are intentionally lowering your frequency, and understand that you have had the wool pulled over your eyes, so to speak, to artificially keep your frequency low.

You see, you are divine beings. You are incredibly creative, powerful beings when you align with love, but when you are out of alignment with love, you become aggressive. You become violent and easily manipulated, and that is indeed what has happened to you.

# CHAPTER 7

# The Seduction of Power

Mentioning things like time travel and portals is, for many of you, an exceptional event in and of itself. We skimmed over that in the last chapter with no intention of leaving it dangling like a juicy piece of information with no backup.

In your society, you have been profoundly deceived about what is really going on. In your long history of contact with extraterrestrial life, those beings found a way to travel from distant planets, distant habitable moons, and even distant dimensions through many different practices. There is the truly nonphysical, which is the consciousness realm of highly evolved beings. That is where we reside, and we share this information with the lower realms because their ignorance causes suffering. We share this information with the lower realms because it is time to reveal these truths.

In your distant past, these truths were revealed. You must remember that long, long ago there were civilizations on this planet that had open communication, open interaction, and open cooperation with beings from other planetary systems, other dimensions, and other times. There are many locations from which beings can emerge or appear to come from. So this past of yours, now shrouded in fear and darkness and ignorance and lies, was a reality for the beings on the planet at that time. There were human societies that were intimately involved with the technologies and the truths about the functioning of your intergalactic brothers and sisters.

Because of the usurpation (or the overtaking) of your psychology a few thousand years ago, you have been intentionally led down the path away from truth, away from expansion, and away from evolution, and this is why you now see your planet devolve into chaos. You have not been allowed to take the path of the naturally evolving consciousness that will always (pay attention to this) choose to feel better. That is what the naturally evolving consciousness does: It chooses an experience, and if that works out, then it pursues more of that experience. It feels good and becomes happier. It expands and raises its frequency, and then it is able to access more information because the frequency issue is always happening. Lower frequency realms are less enjoyable, and higher-frequency realms are more enjoyable. This happens with an animal as simple as a cow. If a cow moves into the hot sun as it grazes and begins to feel a little uncomfortable, it will move into the shade and lie down until the temperature beyond that shaded area decreases. This is a natural response of the physical/material self. It always seeks balance.

So what happened with your structures, particularly with your religious, political, and financial structures, was that they began to use this information, this knowledge about how humans evolve and how they work and how they create. This information came from the higher realms as many beings shared this truth with humanity: If you align with love, then you will increase your power and influence. This is the basic tenant of the teachings we bring forth, the basic tenant of the evolution of consciousness.

Beings of a lower frequency began to influence humanity. They began to influence humans at the top of the pecking order, and they said, "If you do 'this,' then you will be able to control people. If you tell them 'this,' you will be able to manipulate people. If you frighten them and punish them and kill them for not obeying these rules, then you will get double the results. You will become the most powerful influencer of many, many beings." Once beings go from the realm of love into the realm of fear, they lose their ability to tap into their true power, which is a connection to the loving force you call God, or the Divine Benevolent Essence, who rules this many-faceted, multidimensional, multiple-universe experience of consciousness that is taking place.

## There Is No Judgment, Only Options

You might ask yourselves, "Why was this allowed?" Well, this is a freewill zone. Your planet is a freewill zone. That is part of its design, to allow consciousness to explore itself, to allow consciousness to try out different experiments. Many civilizations on your planet did not survive because they did not choose love. They often chose fear, destruction, war, and manipulation as their path. This is downloaded as experience into the greater consciousness of these oversoul structures. You might again ask how this is allowed. Well, that is how evolution happens. It is the God experience, and that is the truth of it. You are allowed to try whatever experiments you want to see how they feel, how much you can learn from them, and whether they work.

From Spirit's and the higher realms' points of view, if a system is tried and fails, that is okay. It is an experience, and those beings who incarnated into that experience will come away from that incarnational journey — that journey into that experiment — with a new way of looking at things. When they are incarnated again, they will try something different because they recall that experiment did not work particularly well.

This is the way it is supposed to work when it is not tampered with, but over the past few thousand years, your minds have been tampered with. That means beings who had this knowledge did not use it to empower you, as we are trying to do. They used it to limit you and to control you and cause you fear, and they actively sought to control everyone on the planet. This is what you saw in your expeditions of Western structures as they disseminated religion in the early part of the Renaissance. This is what happened when Catholic ministers and missionaries headed to other areas.

These were beings who were free, beings who participated in the unregulated experience of consciousness evolution. That means they had developed a society and were experiencing their own evolutions. Some of those societies were violent. Some of those societies took a negative detour, and that was their choice. They learned their own lessons. But these highly evolved beings — we are not saying highly evolved in a good sense; we are saying it in the sense that they are powerful, psychic masters who fully comprehend how the human mind works — began to influence the governments and royal societies of the time to use fear, control, and manipulation as the power structure to bring large numbers of people under control. That is what you saw in the Inquisition. The Inquisition was a systematic and planned psychic domination of the population of that time.

We are going far, far back in your history. Most of you who are conspiracy theorists or believers in these negative hierarchies often do not realize how far back these systems go. They go back thousands and thousands of years. That is why you are so fearful of breaking the rules and of standing out: It has become genetically anchored in your cultural memory. There have been so many generations of fear and control and manipulation that you are literally integrating it into your physical body-mind structures, and that is why it will take time for your consciousness to shift and become empowered once again.

Be very gentle with yourselves as you shift and change regarding these subjects. We want you to know that there has been such a long and determined application of pressure to the human consciousness individually and as a collective that you are going to have difficulty with some of these ideas, some of the proposals we make here, but we cannot force you. We cannot rush you. All we can do is tell you.

For those of you who like to leap ahead and go to the front of the class, this does not work when reconstructing a human consciousness, when you are relearning from the ground up. That is what we are doing in these books. We don't want to belabor the point, but go back to the beginning if you have skipped ahead and this is making you fearful.

## Choose Love

The manipulations that have taken place in your society have deep roots, but the truth is that you are divine aspects of God mind, and you come in with free will. You come in with a powerful consciousness that has the ability to choose, and this is the power that we want to call from you now. You have the ability to choose the opposite of fear, which is a method of control and manipulation.

You can choose love. That was the purpose of the teachings Jesus brought to the Earth plane 2,000 years ago in this particular timeline. (Yes, there are many other timelines, but we are working with this one right now.) In that time and place, his purpose, his dedication to helping humanity, was to bring truth to the planet once again. Even though it seems as though it was long ago in this society's development, there had already been a very negative and manipulative application of mind control on the beings of that time and place, and it was done through war, fear, wealth, and the religious and political structures of the time. Jesus came in as a highly evolved being connected to Divine mind to bring information that would teach those beings how to become free of the physical, material, low-frequency ideas and thoughts and beliefs that they had been taught and were inadvertently using to miscreate on this planet. In the next chapter, we are going to go into the idea of creation and miscreation so that you have a better idea of how these manipulations of fear and control work in your society.

# CHAPTER 8

# Know Your Natural Magnificence

The consciousness in which you find yourself is a magnificent manifestation of the attributes of God. This is not how you are used to seeing yourselves. You undermine yourselves with constant judgments. You attack yourselves for not being better looking or better paid. There are many things you judge yourselves for, and because of these judgments, you disconnect from the awareness of your magnificence. For many of you in this world, the words "you are a divine aspect of God mind, a powerful creator," do not make sense because you have been trained to be victims through the many machinations of your society. We have covered some of these ideas in other books, but we will continue to help you understand what has happened to you through a little repetition.

Thousands of years of teachings are deeply ingrained in the fundamental fabric of your society, and what is your society but a physical manifestation of your consciousness? So when you look out in your world and see societies viciously bombing and attacking each other or you see a society that repeatedly consumes more than it gives to the planet, depleting valuable resources, you do not see that you are part of the problem. You do not see that you are responsible for the negativities around you. You participate in your society. You purchase items these industries produce. You use goods and services that cause pollution. You have been taught that you are powerless. You do not view reality correctly or see that you are, in fact, bringing into being the things that will, in the end, destroy you.

This is a very important part of the structure of the collective-consciousness ego mind in your society. The ego mind is split. That means it does not understand itself. It accuses other beings of doing what it does. That is the "face of innocence" all of you present to the world, the face and the voice that says, "I hate war. I do not want war; I want peace!" Yet there it is, manifesting in the world. This divided structure of your egoic consciousness must be understood to truly comprehend how creation and miscreation work.

## Reclaim Your Power through Forgiveness

Miscreation, which is causing your world to fall into disarray, is the belief that you have nothing to do with what is happening outside you. You do not believe your broken relationships have anything to do with you, and you believe the things you are experiencing are other people's fault. You believe that other people can make you feel bad and that other people can, in fact, hurt you. You have the belief that society has nothing to do with you, and that places you in the role of victim. In that placement, you are powerless.

Now, this belief you hold has been taught to you. Jesus, when he came to Earth so many years ago, taught the opposite of powerlessness. He taught that the kingdom of heaven is within and that each of you is capable of performing the miracles he performed. These are things he said to people and taught his Disciples. They too were healers. They too were able to access the frequencies of knowledge he resided in. This is why he was murdered.

He went to the cross by choice. He had come to the end of his time as a teacher in that particular form, although he continued to teach for many years after the crucifixion, as he describes in *Jesus: My Autobiography* [Light Technology Publishing, 2015]. The truth is that he was taken out of the game, in that physical sense, by the powers that be because he taught independence. He taught how to tap into the powerful realms of love through the practice of forgiveness.

Practicing forgiveness demonstrates that you understand you are a creator. It demonstrates you understand that if you identify something or somebody outside of you as the problem, you are literally attacking the part of your mind that you have put outside you, that split mind, the projection of the egoic consciousness. When you practice forgiveness, you bring your power back to you, and that is the opposite of what the ego believes. When you miscreate, you put all your energy and belief and power outside you even though it is still inside you.

The split mind is not really a split mind but the illusion of a split mind. For example, when you say, "The government is powerful, and I cannot overwhelm it," you continue to give it your power. Your belief — which is your creative ability, the thing that makes you godlike — that the government has power over you and that you can do nothing maintains that illusion. That is what the ego consciousness is; it is the illusion of powerlessness and separation.

The teachings that Jesus brought through and that we are continuing are the truth, but you must believe them to manifest them. The truth is that you have the ability to bring back all your creative power. You bring it back through the practice of forgiveness, which is a demonstration of your understanding that love is always the answer. Love brings the mind into oneness. The mind that is returned to oneness has access to all the power in the universe because that is the frequency of love, which is the frequency of God. So to tune in to God, you must forgive the world and learn to love everything you see. That reunifying action will manifest the healing of your split mind. It will take you up into the frequencies of love and mastery of the physical/material world, and that is what Jesus did. He practiced loving kindness and forgiveness to such a degree that he was no longer separated in mind and therefore was no longer separated from the tremendous power that is available to you.

So the beings who were already in a place of influence and power and financial control — taxation, militarism, these kinds of things — listened to Jesus and understood his teaching. They knew that if the peasants and the workers and the underlings of society were allowed to practice this teaching, those in power would lose control of them. So they put an end to Jesus's teachings. He was okay with it at the time; it was enough. He had done enough in the physical form as it expressed itself in that time and place. His work continues. It has never stopped, but it changed form.

Those beings took those influential teachings alignment with love, and they edited, manipulated, and rewrote them to create the Christian church. The Roman Catholic Church distorted and edited the teachings of Jesus and used them against the population through retribution and fearful, limiting, and restrictive ideas that the church knew would disempower the people and lower their frequency from the realm of creative genius to the realm of miscreation. That is what you are seeing in your society. You are seeing the result of 2,000 years of miscreation.

## Retrain Your Mind through Love

When you are a divine aspect of God mind, you always have free will, and you always have access to Divine Mind, to Spirit. This is a constant battle these hierarchies that know how creation works must wage generation after generation because each time a being comes into form on this planet, he or she comes with tremendous creative ability, and this ability never leaves him or her. It can, however, be masked by beliefs and indoctrination and teachings that cause that person to look in the wrong direction. This is where religious teachings of the past, the current school systems, and (increasingly) social media and mass media programming systems are guiding you. They have always taken the form of fear. In your religious histories, it was fear of the devil, spiritual possession, and the flesh. These were all prohibitions to keep you away from your sacredness and your connection to the Divine.

As you traveled through time, these messages changed form, but the frequency was the same, and as you move into your technological, highly modern world, these hateful messages and limiting beliefs and ideas now reside in the advertising and mass marketing systems penetrating your mind each moment through your phones, televisions, and computers. They are constantly indoctrinating you into limitation, and they are constantly indoctrinating you into materialism. In the realm of materialism, you remain powerless.

For example, in motorcar advertising, you see that if you drive a certain car, you will become attractive to the opposite sex. If you believe that message, then you literally hand your power and influence over to the car, and you become more and more fractured. This happens with every item you purchase. With every belief in the material that you engage with in your heart and mind, you become less and less influential. In your mind, you are still influential, but you miscreate, which means you manufacture a fearful world from a fearful place. You manufacture an unloving word from an unloving place because the belief in materialism is a very low-frequency belief, and love is a high-frequency belief. This is why the great masters have always taught loving kindness and forgiveness as the path to awakening. In that practice, you raise your frequency out of the realm of materialism.

This has been going on for such a long time in your society that you have become blind to it. Generation after generation has swallowed these deceptions hook, line, and sinker. You look back and see your parents and your grandparents doing it, so there is a long line of seeming truths that, in fact, are lies. The lies appear to be truth, and the truth that you are a godlike creator appears to be a lie. You look at your sick bodies, warring countries, and financial poverty (or lack) and you say, "I am no God. I am not powerful. Look at me; I cannot even pay my rent easily. I am sick, I am not happy, and I have to go to a job I don't like!" These are all demonstrations of your belief in your powerlessness, and that is the most horrendous inheritance from generation after generation of beings who are separated from the true nature of their magnificence.

Now you begin to understand what is happening in your world. Now you see how violence is generated. Now you see how entire generations of people can believe they have no strength and no ability to assert themselves. This is a very challenging aspect of these teachings because you have been trained in duality, war, and materialism, and we must ask you to be very patient as you retrain yourselves.

We bring these books through in a particular order so that you can retrain your minds systematically and safely into a more expanded version because only in the more expanded version will you be able to manifest the world you want. This is how your stories of the Holocaust cause great dysfunction in your society, and repeating the terror that it could happen again guarantees it will. When you focus on something, that is what comes, that is what the terrorized, victimized mind manufactures. When you believe that an entire race of beings can be victimized without contributing to it through the frequency they hold, you demonstrate that you do not understand the laws of creation.

This is where your minds must change. You must accept that your life is your creation. You must accept that you demonstrate an error of thought when you suffer or when you are out of accord with abundance, health, or financial well-being. You demonstrate that you do not have a conscious, aware, integrated connection with the divine aspect of mind, which is your source of wealth and healing and abundance.

You are divine aspects of God mind and very powerful indeed, but when your mind is focused in the wrong direction or in the wrong frequency, you become quite dangerous. You are experiencing the dangers of your collective, powerful minds manipulated into looking the wrong way. The wrong way is war; the wrong way is away from love. The wrong way is judgment and materialism. The right way is peace, the right way is love, and the right way is kindness. The right way is generosity and forgiveness. Knowing this is the only way you will get back the tremendous influence and power that is your natural right, the gift you all received from that divine, benevolent force you call God.

# CHAPTER 9

# The Danger of Projection

There is no linear, logical, physical explanation for murder. This is an insane aspect of the ego mind. What this does is place the secret, which is the thing being driven by savagery wants, in the body of the person who is being killed. This is a strange concept, that one being would perceive another being holds a secret inside that can be retrieved through murder.

This story makes no sense when you look at it that way, but the truth is when you kill a body, you seek to release from it the thing you want. You seek to release from it the thing you believe it has that you do not have. Just think about this for a moment. Why else would you kill somebody? You believe his or her body holds something away from you that you want or need. This is always the motivation behind murder. If you believe a body contains the secret you want or need, you must either have that body or destroy it.

This is the fundamental teaching of the ego. The body holds a secret, and you must get it. But this is not the truth. It is an illusory distortion of thought and belief. That is what transpired in the Holocaust of the 1940s, and it is what transpires in any attack on the body. You believe that the body is the culprit. You believe that the body is the problem, and this is the grand projection that plays out on your Earth plane all the time. For example, when you are unhappy, you believe your body is the problem. If only it were better looking, heavier, thinner, curvier, or more muscular, whatever it is you decide. You think the body is the problem, so you seek to transform it, but a greater issue is at play, such as fear or control. When you perceive another person's body as the issue, you attack it.

A body only acts based on the thoughts that the mind in it believes. Even in that sentence, there is a misperception, but we are using your language. You believe that minds are contained within bodies. The truth is that bodies are contained within minds. Bodies are created by minds, and bodies are motivated by minds. This is the basic premise you must get before you can understand bad behavior. Bad behavior, such as killing people, is a motivation of the mind. It does not have anything to do with a body, and in this understanding, you will be able to practice forgiveness because you will see that a body cannot behave any differently than it is asked to behave by the mind that motivates it just as you cannot behave out of accord with a belief you have. If you love dogs, you cannot hurt dogs. If you hate dogs, you can hurt dogs. This is the behavior aspect you deal with in every incarnation.

You generally don't think of things in this way, that bodies are seen as the culprit, but that is what the Holocaust was. It was a mind — the mind of Adolf Hitler — that perceived the bodies of other beings as guilty. He did not perceive the minds of those beings at all. That was the motivation behind the assassination of so many bodies. He believed in the physical/material world as the most important place. The most important place is the mind.

The mind must change for behavior to change. Hitler was involved in the physical/material world as the source of his feelings, and this is projection. He sought to attain a feeling by destroying other bodies. He sought to attain power through the destruction of other bodies, and this arose from a dysfunctional mind, an insane mind.

## Violence Begets Violence

What you see in the Middle East is an insane action perpetrated on innocence by a distorted consciousness being used for justification for further insanity. And this is difficult for you to understand at this time, but the insane mind of the one you know as Hitler, the insane and clever mind that learned to manipulate and control other minds, will not happen again unless you continue to focus on it. This is happening in your society. You have been trained that this will happen again if you do not become rigid and controlling and focus on the insane behavior carried out in those years. What you are witnessing in the Middle East is that insane behavior being created again because that is what you focus on. It is a perfect demonstration of a mind creating something and another mind judging it and therefore re-creating it.

This is why your world looks like hell. This is why when viciousness, war, and violence are used to correct, it turns so horribly wrong time after time. By attacking the being who attacked, you are aligning with the same energy. You say, "You killed, so we will kill." You become the same insane destroyer of bodies that you claim to hate. This is why war never works as a solution to a problem. You are, in fact, dealing with the same level of frequency — with the insane egoic consciousness — that kills bodies in an effort to prevent killing bodies. You read this sentence and realize it is insane. So in the Middle East, through this repetitive storytelling, a justification for murder is playing out. In this chaotic Middle Eastern system, you see the result of decade after decade of using violence as a solution to violence, and the beings who fear the monster become the monster. They have taken on the frequency of insanity, the frequency of the killer, and the frequency of the Third Reich in this time and place.

## War Is Never the Solution

Saying these words is taboo in your society. It is considered dangerous because the strategic use of this story of the Holocaust has been used to manipulate you and to justify war and the horrendous acts taking place in the Middle East. The Middle East is a powerful vortex on your planet. It contains many time portals used to move people and objects and supplies into other areas of your solar system and even your star system. This is not mainstream news in your world. It is not news that is allowed. The situation in the Middle East is so chaotic and makes no sense because the story you are getting is not the truth. The story you are getting has been long in the making, and it is being used to facilitate the capture and control of these access points within your star system.

These truths about time travel and the existence of portals will surprise many of you who have happily followed our teachings based on your concepts of spirituality, but we must tell you the truth about your planet.

We must tell you the truth about what is really going on; otherwise, you will be lost in a dreamworld, and you will not react appropriately to the information coming to you over the next few years.

In the next few years, your society will learn that a manipulative and controlling global hierarchy has been messing with you for a very long time, and if you don't get the truth, if you don't get the correct lens through which to view this unfolding, you will become enraged and violent. Remember, you have been trained to be violent. You have been trained to use aggression as a solution despite the many hundreds of years of evidence that this does not work and despite the millions of deaths that have occurred throughout the centuries when war is employed as a solution.

The beings in control love war; it is the food for their energy systems. They are not like you. They do not thrive on love. They thrive on the absence of love, which is fear. They have used this motivation to control you because when you are fearful, they are happy, they are powerful, and they can continue manipulating you. When you are in the frequency of love and you practice forgiveness, when you raise yourself out of these limited physical realms, you become more powerful than they are because love is always more powerful than fear. When love enters a room, it is like light entering the darkness: it changes it forever. So those of you who have been counseled in violence, indoctrinated in shooting, and taught to judge are giving away your power and influence in every moment you make those choices. We must bring you the truth that these choices feed the negative systems that control your planet.

Those negative systems have you firmly in their grasp because of the education system you have been through. It teaches you to never stand out, punishes you if you make errors, and teaches you to value yourself based on the opinions of others. All these mechanisms are used to maintain control over you when you reach adulthood. Many of you are outraged by what is happening on your planet, yet you sit on your couches completely compliant, wringing your hands and saying, "This is terrible! This is terrible!" but you do not stand up to do anything about it. You believe you are powerless. You are an individual, and you are a physical body. You are the powerhouse that drives the culture in which you live. You are the creator of everything you witness, and you are doing it unconsciously.

## When You Focus on the Past, You Re-create It

Now, we have thrown in some very interesting information in this chapter about the Holocaust, the Middle East, and your manipulation. You must back away from the traditional way of viewing the Holocaust. You must understand that an insane person who killed millions of bodies and who was very intelligent and manipulative is being used to perpetrate insanity of the same kind, of the same value, in the Middle East at this time. When you look at it this way, you will begin to change your mind, and in changing your mind, you will disempower the systems that use your fear and your anger at the Holocaust as fuel for another holocaust.

You must change your mind and say, "Enough of that old story! We must tell a new story here. We must bring love to the subject. We must forget the past and create a new future from this moment." Until you are willing to do that, willing to forgive that horrific event in the past, you will bring the same energy into the present moment, and then you will be guaranteed another holocaust. There is another holocaust taking place at this time in the Middle East because of this story that has been told a million times.

There are those of you from that time and place, from that generation, who say Hitler had to be stopped. He did have to be stopped, but other ways of stopping him could have been implemented much earlier than the vicious attacks of World War II. World War II killed almost an entire generation of young men, and your society is still reeling from that loss. But the greater loss is the continued hatred of Hitler. Hitler has moved on in his incarnations and is reaping the rewards of the seeds he sowed not in hatred, not in judgment from Spirit, but in forgiveness and in love. He is loved by Spirit. He took your society on a journey into negativity with lessons that are being lost because of the repeated manipulations around that story.

If these stories had not been manipulated and this event had not been used, every being that was involved in the Holocaust — the soldiers, the murderers, the organizers, and the victims — would have moved on from that incarnation and would have retrieved from it an experience that informed him or her about love, death, murder, retribution, healing, and many other things. Each being would have had his or her combination of understandings from the experience, and he or she would have brought that into the next incarnation, clearly employing whatever it was that person had learned in that next physical incarnation.

Now, because you have been manipulated by the controllers of the war machine, the lessons and the energy of that story are repeating. When you focus on past wars, on past injuries, you re-create them because they have not been forgiven. They demonstrate the separated ego consciousness. That is what war and fighting do: They demonstrate the ego mind's belief in separation. If you focus on that year after year after year, which is what you have been taught to do pertaining to the Holocaust, then you bring that energy back day after day after day. It is fed day after day after day and will manifest again in a holocaust.

This is what you are seeing in these Middle Eastern countries being devastated by war. The situation is being created by those of you who hold on to the Holocaust as the ultimate unforgivable crime. As long as you, as a collective, believe that story, you are destined to repeat it. If you raise yourselves into the realm of forgiveness with this story, then you will begin to heal the Middle East. You will begin to bring love into the consciousness of that area because the Holocaust story is being used to justify murder, to justify the terrible behavior of murdering bodies.

We want you to know that this story about the Holocaust — the movies you watch about it and the memorials you have to it — feeds the energy of death. It feeds the energy of fear and the current wars that are taking place there. You are the people who will decide whether or not this devastating method of control will continue. You are the ones who must take back your minds and forgive the unforgivable. Only in forgiving the unforgivable will you create a new world.

Next we will lay out some of the specifics of this story. We will give some examples of lessons on expansion and fear and growth and forgiveness, and we will tell you how this works so that you can use these principles in your own lives in your own way.

# CHAPTER 10

# Forgive the Violence
# of the Holocaust

The way you view the Holocaust is the way you view your future, and we really want to impress this on you as you read. Until you forgive that event, until you take your gaze from the past, you will not be able to change the future. Your focus on the past and your constant reiteration of those crimes — holding them up as justification for further crimes — are creating the hell you see in the Middle East. Humans are not taught how creation and reincarnation work and that the mechanisms of those devices, even the most horrific experience or occurrence, can work to benefit humanity.

Millions and millions of souls experienced losing their lives in that time and place you know as World War ll. The beings who were designated as the victims in that drama chose to be victims in that drama, and the beings who were the perpetrators, controllers, and manipulators chose that role too so that they could have a particular experience. This is offensive to the structures in your mind that believe in victimization as a passive act. Those of you who believe victims truly are victims and all of you who believe in the Holocaust and promote its memory are such beings. All of you who agree that you have no power to stop the person hurting you are playing out that same game.

In writing these books about the truth of how creation works, we are breaking your rules, and we will upset you. We will say things that go against everything you have been taught, and it will seem as if we are the bad guys. We ask you to look around your world. How is your system working? How are you all doing here? How does the future look for your society? We must ask you these questions to get you out of your arrogance in believing that you know how to look at this situation. You do not know how to look at this situation because you have been trained incorrectly.

You have not been taught about reincarnation, and you have not been taught about how Spirit educates itself, so you fall for the lies of the manipulators who know how powerful your minds are. We keep going back to this because it is the motivation for the poor education systems and the repeated indoctrination in hatred that fuels the wars on your planet. You are trained to provide the energy for those systems, which is what these beliefs you hold are doing.

## Your Experiences Reflect Your Beliefs

Before any being is born in a physical body, it is helped to design a life that will bring it experiences that it does not yet have a complete understanding of. This is taking place out of time with a consciousness that knows it is eternal and the counsel of beings of much higher frequency who have the consciousness evolution of that being as their highest purpose. Money is not their purpose. Influence is not their purpose. The education and expansion of the being coming into physical manifestation is their purpose. When they counsel this being, that is what they have in mind and what the being has in mind because the being coming into consciousness wants to grow, learn, and understand. It wants to comprehend, and it must do that through experience. This is the only way that beliefs can be changed — through experience.

You will experience this. If you read a book written by another consciousness, you get a different point of view, a different image of an experience, but you don't get the experience. You can read a story about going to war and feel it and imagine the images as you read it, but you are not getting the actual experience.

To evolve consciousness, the physical body-mind structure must have an actual experience; otherwise, you could evolve just by reading, and that is not the case. You must evolve by experiencing, so it is important for beings to understand the depth and width and texture and taste and frequency of every experience. So it is with great courage, at times, that a spirit will decide to go in as the bad guy. This is as difficult a job as going in as the victim. Now why, you might ask, do people have to go in as victims or attackers at all? Well, the truth is you don't, but you believe in these things.

When a human mind believes in victimization and attack, that is what it must create. In this time and place on this physical Earth plane, as long as you believe in attack and defense and victims and perpetrators, you will re-create that in your future. You are the creator of your future lives based on the beliefs you hold and act on in this one. The beliefs that you truly, viscerally believe in this one will be what are created in the next one. Why? It is not a punishment. You simply must experience what you believe until you change your mind.

If your belief is out of accord with love but you still believe it, you are given the freedom to believe it lifetime after lifetime until you have an experience that changes your mind. This brings us to the story of the victim and the perpetrator. If you believe in attacking as a solution, then you will become an attacker in your next life. If you believe that you are powerless, that you have no influence in the world, then you will come in as a victim, and you will experience that belief until you change your mind. That is all any incarnation is for.

In the Holocaust, a huge group of spirits came in to help evolve human consciousness. All those beings came in as the victims and the perpetrators, and before they came in, they said, "Let us all do this at the same time. Let us make a huge group of victimizers and a huge group of victims, and the world will pay attention. We will get their attention, and instead of repeating this victim-victimizer game in the small realms of marriages and families, people will come to a deeper understanding of how horrific being an attacker is and how horrific being a victim is. The message and the demonstration of this will be so huge that humanity will pay attention to it. In paying attention to it, they will learn the horrors of war and attack, and they will stop it. They will learn that it does not bring anything but horrific results."

That was the intention of all the beings who came in that manifestation in that time and place. Their hearts were in the right place. All the people who had believed in victimizing became victimizers once again, and all the beings who believed they were victims came in as victims once again, but they did it in such a huge group that they believed, at the time, designing that particular experience would help heal humanity.

### Distractions of Fear and Violence Keep You from Love

Your society's leaders know the principles of creation, and they understand how to manipulate minds. They understand good and lack of good, which is what you call evil. Good is aligned with love, kindness, generosity, sharing, and compassion. Lack of love manifests as death, disease, murder, hatred, jealousy, and violence. The beings who rule your world at this time understand this, and they know that if they keep you focused on violence, you will not be able to reach love, you will not be able to reach compassion, and you will not be able to expand into the greater being you are. So the story of the Holocaust was repeatedly perpetrated on your minds not as the lesson in love that it was intended to be from the beings who participated in it but as a manipulation of your frequency to keep you aligned with hatred, war, and murder.

That is why you are seeing such a devastating increase in war in your society. You have repeated the stories of the Holocaust, and nobody is allowed to question it. Nobody is allowed to bring in another opinion of what it might mean, as we are doing. That is why many violent movies and video games are being marketed to you, pushed on you. It is a concerted effort to align you with hatred, war, and killing because that serves the energy requirements that rule your planet at this time.

That is the truth. We will explain how reincarnation truly works so that you grasp the fundamental structure of the evolution of your consciousness. But we want you to know that every one of those beings came in knowing he or she was doing a service for the greater good of humanity. It has been hijacked, however, as many of the good, humanitarian, kind acts have been on your world at this time.

This is why these interventions are happening now, and yes, Spirit is intervening in your world. Beings are asserting themselves, finally, because you are losing your ability to create a good future. You are losing your ability to align with love because you are trained to align with hatred, violence, and war throughout your lives. By the time you reach adulthood, you have become very dangerous people because of the way you use your minds. That is why we are here. We are here to help explain how your mind works: The frequency it holds creates the physical experience, and when you align with those frequencies, you are destined to be hurt lifetime after lifetime. Your children are destined to be hurt lifetime after lifetime if you keep teaching them hatred and violence and that the past is real.

The past only becomes creative when you bring it into the present moment, and that is what all these Holocaust memorials do. They repeatedly bring insanity and hatred back into the present, and you must forgive that most horrific experience, the one that was designed to teach you not to be attackers and not to be victims. That lesson is being lost every time you believe the Holocaust was an unforgivable sin, the Nazis were unforgivably evil, and the Jews were powerless victims. Every one of those beliefs keeps those untruths alive, and until you forgive it and comprehend how it was meant to work, you will participate in that perpetuation of hatred and war that you are seeing manifest in front of your eyes in the Middle East.

# CHAPTER 11

# Read the Writing
# on the Wall

The concerns you have as you read this book are that you will be a bad person somehow if you don't reflect on the Holocaust as a disaster and offer sympathy to the survivors or the images that you see from your news media, documentary films, and these kinds of things. You will also fear persecution. You will fear that if you say something differently than you normally would, people around you will accuse you of being anti-Semitic, or they might accuse you of being a Nazi. These are some of the greatest insults people can hurl at each other in your society, and this too is part of the plan.

The powers that be thought this out very well. Through your school systems, they have taught you to conform. Through your church systems, they have taught you the need to sacrifice and suffer, and they have taught you the current belief that any Jew on this planet must fight for survival and must use war and machine guns and whatever weapons are available to prevent being killed by a "Hitler" again. These seeds that were planted in your minds long ago play into your fears.

As we reveal a different point of view to you, we want you to know that when you hold a profound, indoctrinated belief for a very long time and a new idea comes to your mind, the mind does not like it. It does not like having something come in that is counter to its indoctrination, so it will try to get back to peace. It must eliminate one of the conflicting notions. Obviously, if you have an indoctrinated belief for forty or fifty years, the Johnny-come-lately information will be the one ousted. That is what your mind will want to do. But bear with us on this story. At this stage of your evolution on your planet, if you do what your mind tells you to do, which is to get rid of this "lie" because this notion is unloving or counterproductive or dangerous, you will not get the information you need to transform your world.

### Forgive in the Eternal Now

You all know that the Middle East is a disaster. You know that innocent people are being murdered and bombed and abused, but your societal teachings convince you that you are powerless to do anything about it. We aren't telling you to hit the streets and demonstrate or to post anything on your Facebook pages so that you can avoid being seen as anti-Semitic or revolutionary in any way. What we are asking you to do is change your mind. We are asking you to think about what we are telling you for a little while.

Contemplate that perhaps the way you have been told this story, the way you have been repeatedly molded by this story, is not serving you or your planet, and it is certainly not serving the beings in the Middle East who are suffering so. The wars are escalating, and the control and manipulation of your media by the warmongers is causing more and more profound suffering. That is going to stop, but we want you to change your minds as this process progresses; otherwise, it will repeat. If you do not change your minds about the past, if you do not forgive it, it is doomed to repeat. The quote you have — "Those who cannot remember the past are condemned to repeat it" [George Santayana] — is actually not true.

We suggest you learn by looking at the past once. Say, "Well, we won't do this again. We will change our behavior and our focus, and we will not do this again!" The relentless marketing of hatred, war, and violence combined with the misleading teaching that if you keep looking at the past it won't repeat actually results in the opposite. If you keep looking to the past, it will repeat because you bring that hatred and insanity and obsession with death into the present and create it again in the only place you can create anything, which is the eternal now.

It is in the eternal now that forgiveness takes place. It is in the eternal now that your future is created. It is not created from the past unless you bring it into the eternal now. That is where everything happens. The eternal now is where you hate, the eternal now is where you love, the eternal now is where we forgive, and the eternal now is where you decide on everything. There is no other time and place. You know this! Every moment that you are aware of yourself is the eternal now. This is the only place you can do anything.

These principles we speak about are very important, much more important, in fact, than the events, the forms of these other things, the wars, the conversations, and the accusations. These are the form of principles. The form of your society is that warring and attacking get you what you want. That is exactly what Hitler did. This is the thing you are missing in your presumptuousness. In saying that you deplore his actions, you are, in fact, repeating them, and that is the absolute irony of this experience you are having. You have become the torturers, the murderers, the invaders, and the empire that he had. You have become that. Of course you have become it. How can you not become it if that is what you have been taught to think?

Now, some of you will say, "Well, I have heard about the Holocaust, and I've heard about Nazi Germany, but I don't think about it all the time." Of course you don't think about it all the time. But you see it, you know it, and you have been indoctrinated by your society to not ever question it, to not ever say anything about it that could go against the general theme of your society's dogma about that particular event.

As soon as you picked up this book, you knew you would read something that would break the rules. You felt it deep inside. "Should I buy this book? Is it going to get me in trouble?" Where did those ideas come from? They come from society indoctrinating you into believing what has become a sacred cow.

## Remove Your Blindfold

As we journey through this experience of exposing the truth about how you have been manipulated, we want you to know that we do not want you to become angry, fearful, or paranoid. What we want you to become is educated. We want you to truly comprehend how your mind works. It is the creator of your body, your experience, your emotions, and your life, and it is the collective experience of your planet that is being created by each of you.

The powers that be have been in charge for a very long time, and they know how to manipulate you. They have been very good at it for a very long time. Century after century, they have practiced oppressing people, buying and selling people, abusing people, and manipulating people, and they have done it behind closed doors. Now there is a revolution on your planet, and the secret societies, secret activities, and hidden agendas are being exposed around the world. It is time for all of you to rework your minds. If you do not begin to change your minds, then the transformations your society is going through will be impossible for you because you will be lost in the past, wishing you could go back to the way things were, when in fact the past was a prison that was limiting and unfair, and it caused a lot of suffering.

The new world will have a much leveler playing field across societies, not just in your Western society. You are very ethnocentric. When you think about equality, you only think about it in your culture, but we are speaking about equality across the board, including the Middle Eastern countries you look at as violent and savage, and the Asian countries you look at as overpopulated and underdeveloped. There will be a more level playing field across the world, and these distortions of Western mind must be addressed because they are the fundamental cause of some of the disparities you see on this planet.

This is a very important time in your society. It is the end of a long cycle of evolution, and what you haven't achieved is coming home to roost very soon. This is not a threat or a god punishing you; it is just one of the natural cycles of your societal and planetary evolution. Just as a tree goes through the spring, summer, autumn, and winter, that natural cycle is not forced on the tree by anyone from the outside. The seasons naturally arise from within the system. That is what is happening on your planet because of your shortsightedness and ignorance. It is not your fault; it has been kept from you. You have lost sight of the cycles of planets, the cycles of seasons, and at times, the cycles of your body, and now these are going to assert themselves in ways that cannot be mistaken.

You live in a baby society — a very young society, relatively speaking — that has been kept in the dark. Imagine a child raised wearing a blindfold. When you take the blindfold off the child, he or she will not know what to do. The child will stumble and fall even though he or she can see more clearly than when the blindfold was on. The child will not know what to do with the information. That is the state that you are in. Your blindfold is about to be taken off, and we are trying to prepare you for what you will see. We are trying to help you take the blindfold off little by little.

## Begin a Revolution Within

Now it is still up for grabs, the absolute unfolding of this revelation, but you must take to heart what we are saying: The fundamental structure of your minds is problematic and the fundamental structure of your belief in good and evil is problematic. The way you look at good people and bad people — terrorists, activists — is fundamentally flawed, and you must be willing to admit this. Admit that what you have been doing hasn't been working. Admit that there must be a better way. Admit that something is going on in your society. None of the people you know want war. All the people you know want environmentally sound power systems. All the people you know abhor violence. All the people you know want organic food widely available, but it is not happening. Why?

There is, in fact, a conspiracy against health and growth — not in the industrial sense, but in the spiritual sense. There is a conspiracy against you becoming the fully realized being we are encouraging you to become. You must see that the way you are educated and raised is the problem that causes your Earth to teeter on the edge of disaster. We will reveal some more secrets and interesting tidbits that will help you expand your minds, your hearts, and your ability to forgive. The dysfunction of your individual minds, through no fault of your own, creates the society you see. It is in your fears, your limitations, your prejudices, and your belief in the material over love. It is in your belief in convenience over perfection or effort. These are some things that miscreate in your society, and we want you to begin to question.

Ask, "Is this the only way there is to live?" Look around your planet. You will see many cultures that have differing values, systems of governance, and ways of being, but they are slowly and surely assimilating to the West through cell phones and televisions and satellites and so on. The West is infecting the entire world. Indigenous cultures and individuality are being annihilated through this indoctrination.

Unplug your phones as often as you can. Unplug your televisions and remove them from your homes. Be careful what movies you watch. If they are filled with violence about good overcoming evil, you are perpetuating the duality of this world, you are perpetuating the war in this world, and you are perpetuating violence as a solution, which you are seeing in this world in many different forms.

Read the writing on the wall: If you keep doing what you're doing, you will not survive. If you keep doing what you are doing, you will suffer more and more as your world deteriorates under repressive regimes.

Begin the revolution within you. That is where it must take place because that is where the contamination and the hypnosis have taken place: in your minds and in your hearts. You must reclaim your minds and hearts. You don't have to tell anyone you are doing it, and you don't have to demonstrate it in any way or any action, but you must focus on love and on forgiveness of the most horrendous crime in your history, the Holocaust.

If you look around honestly, you will see that there is another holocaust at play, and it is the evil twin of the Holocaust. It has come into being because the other has duplicated itself through your creative abilities, through the power of your thinking.

# CHAPTER 12

# Match Your Frequency
# to Gaia's

Your destiny is being decided. This opportunity for expansion is the most important moment in the history of your planet. Many societies were on your planet before the one you live in. They have been hidden from you, and they have disappeared into legend, such as Atlantis and Lemuria. These places have names, but they have been described as mythological. People have been ridiculed for believing they existed. You are experiencing the repetition of an egoic pattern. When a society is engaged in separation, it is perpetually choosing between good and bad: attacking each other, judging each other, pointing out differences, disrespecting each other, or worshiping each other. These are the many facets of the uninformed separation experience.

Earth is a sentient being. She is Gaia, a wise and generous and fertile and productive being who has allowed you to populate her surface. She brings forth a frequency of love, generosity, kindness, and abundance and provides prolific genetic material for you to play with, eat, and join with. A shift in frequency is happening on this planet, the being on which you live.

You are not taught about this. You have been told that these planetary bodies, these orbs in the solar system, are inanimate objects even though they teem with life, have obvious natural systems, and ebb and flow. You have been indoctrinated with the untruth that your planet has no feelings, no soul, and no self-determination. This is, in fact, one of the biggest lies of your time taught to you because it was imperative that you allow the industrial complex. You had to believe that this planet had no feelings or any kind of innate value or soul so that you would not feel for her as oil was drilled and pollution was expelled with impunity.

Earth has had enough of your games. She is moving into a new phase of her evolution just as spring moves to summer and summer moves to autumn and autumn moves to winter. You have natural cycles. Well, the planetary bodies have their own journeys into expansion and evolution, and Earth — Gaia, this beautiful mother on which you have been residing in ignorance — is moving on to her next phase, her next season, and it is one of a higher frequency. That means the lower frequencies that have been imposed on you from the hierarchical systems ruling the planet for the past few thousand years will no longer be tolerated. They won't be dispatched through any action, necessarily, but through a dissonance between the frequencies.

## Stand Up and Raise Your Frequency

When you have a low frequency and a high frequency resonating together, one must change. Either the lower frequency must rise to the higher one, or the higher one will slow to match the lower one. You are less powerful than Gaia. She is much stronger than you. She has been here for a very long time and will continue to be here for a very long time. She has the more powerful influence in this equation, and you must catch up with her.

Because of the lies and the deception that have been perpetrated against you in your society, you are in what we call the remedial class. You have been kept behind a few grades, and your frequency is not where it should be. If you had been out in nature growing your own food and being educated by wisdom teachings and wise teachers, you would have adjusted upward over the past few hundred years to Gaia's frequency. But because of your indoctrination and mechanizations and urbanization, you have separated from the natural frequencies. You have become ignorant and dangerously ill informed, and you are not doing well in catching up to her.

What does this have to do with the Nazi regime? Well, the indoctrination and teachings you have about it are being used to keep you artificially low in frequency. So when a bomb is dropped in the Middle East and you question it, the argument comes back about Israel and about Hitler and how this cannot be allowed to happen again. So these warmongering, militaristic systems are given a free pass because you have been taught not to question anything about the Holocaust. The methodology in trying to prevent it from happening again is not working. It is, in fact, creating another holocaust, and you are all standing on the sidelines in your fearfully indoctrinated minds, refusing to step up and say something.

Regardless of the billions of dollars that are sent to these centers to create more and more disturbance and more and more war, your conditioning programs keep you silent with your hands over your mouths, terrified to say anything. The low frequency of war is therefore allowed to continue, and you inadvertently contribute to that low frequency in your ignorance.

We are here to take off that gag. We are here to take off the blindfold you have been wearing. You must stand up internally to reveal (first to yourself and then to other beings) that this methodology is unacceptable, that isolating beings in Palestine and bombing them is unacceptable. These are war crimes against humanity. Arming a country and pointing missiles all over the place in preparation for intended war is not acceptable.

You cannot stand up and raise your frequency into the realms of peace and love until you face this demon in your culture. This is a lie that has been perpetrated on you — not that the Holocaust did not happen, but that you must continue to arm yourselves against the potential that it will be repeated. It is happening again for those poor beings in the Middle East. It is hell to live in that place, and those beings need you to speak up. They need you, the educated and influential Western person, to stand up energetically, mentally, and emotionally within yourself, and then they need you to stand up in real time with words and actions and a shift in your beliefs about how to solve these problems.

As you enter into this very powerful time in your society, know you are the ones who will be responsible for changing this frequency to keep up with Gaia in her evolutionary process. Why have you been kept ignorant? It has served the purposes of those beings who have been in charge of you. Why did they manipulate your consciousness? It served their purposes. It allowed them to harvest minerals, oil, and even energy from you.

The powers that be thrive on fear and confusion and hatred. That is their food, their energy source. They are not like you. They are a different breed. They are a different culture and genetic makeup. A human must be loved or he or she will die. If you put a child in an orphanage and do not touch and love him or her, that child will literally die. Humans need love to survive. These beings do not need love; in fact, they need fear to survive.

The insanity that rules on your planet — the society that you look at and shake your head at and wonder, "How did we get here?" — is thriving in their opinion. The beings that rule your world are thriving because of pollution, environmental degradation, fear, and war. That is their nutrition, and that is why you see the ruling elite of this planet perpetuating war year after year. When they can keep you in a state of disruption, fear, and confusion, they are full with the food that they crave. Now, these are not principles and ideas that you are used to hearing about, but the jig is up, dear ones. It is time to truly understand what is happening. If you don't, you cannot make the changes required for your survival.

## Choose Your Internal Transformation

We have been taking you on an energetic journey to a place where you will be able to take back your power and create what you want, which is a loving society. However, you must fully understand that the society you are witnessing is taking your financial and energetic resources and your happiness. There are societies around this planet that are suffering so profoundly that this intervention has been decided.

The intervention comes from the nonphysical. Ascended masters — highly evolved conscious beings of your time and space — have come together to help you shift your consciousness so that you can match that of your planet. She is going on her own evolutionary journey into a much higher frequency, and to join her, you must know the truth. You must know what has been done to you. You must know what to do. The Holocaust, this never-ending story of trauma and torture, must be put to rest through the practice of forgiveness.

So as you read, feel all the fears, all the confusion, and all the "I mustn't say anything about this" going on inside you. We want you to feel it. We want you to take notes about what you think will happen if you say anything, what you think will happen to the world if this warmongering stops, and what you think will happen to your governments or your countries. These are all insidious seeds of terror that have been implanted in your society decade after decade, and you must be willing to ask the questions.

You don't have to tell anyone else what you are doing, but to begin this process, you must question these practices. You must say, "If there is a spiritual world out there, if there is some kind of karmic balancing system, then the Holocaust was for a grand purpose. It was to show us something. It was designed with love behind it." This is the hardest thing for you to understand after the teachings you have had and the conditioning programs that are active in your consciousness: The beings who came in as perpetrators chose that role, and the beings who came in as victims chose that role. They did it so that you could have the grandest lesson in why not to victimize, why not to hate, why not to be passive, and why not to be overly empowered. These were the lessons of the Holocaust, and until you see that, accept it, and let it go, knowing they are the lessons and you need to employ them in your thoughts, beliefs, and eventually your words and actions, then you will be in a powerless place because you are being played as the system unfolds right now. You are being played, your energies and money are being siphoned off, and the tremendous wealth of this planet is being extricated by beings who do not care about your future, your happiness, your wealth, or your well-being.

Now is the time to begin your internal transformation. There are great forces that manifest in physical life, and they give you the opportunity to grow and learn. That is what the Holocaust was for. It was designed by those beings who participated in it to give you the ultimate lesson in love and compassion and kindness. It was not designed to perpetuate war. It was not designed to be used forevermore as a justification for brutality, rape, and murder; it was not designed for that. It has been used against you, and you are all paying the price. The dear beings in the Middle East are paying the price for this untruth that has been perpetuated in your society.

Now is the time to ask questions, and as we go through this book, we bring up ways that you can do that without frightening yourself and upsetting other people. We show you how to heal your consciousness, and in that healing, you will raise your frequency enough to take the journey into higher consciousness with Gaia.

She does not care whether you come or not. She is moving through her process, so it must be your decision. She is not going to encourage you or ask you to join her. She is fine without you, and she will go on her excursion into higher consciousness. We suggest you go with her. It will be a very nice ride once you get there, but you must know how to let go of the past. You must reeducate yourself mentally, emotionally, and spiritually, and you must understand that your governments and ruling elites have been manipulating you. You have been fed a story, and you took the bait. Now you are paying the price for it.

# CHAPTER 13

# How to Help Yourselves

A s you go through these chapters, take breaks if you need to, cry if you need to, and write in a journal if you need to. Do not rush through any of this information. It is important that you maintain your mind's integrity at this stage of your planet's evolution. As these stories are revealed to you in the mainstream news (although most of this is going to come out in what you consider alternative media) piece by piece by piece, this material will really help you integrate it into your consciousness.

The things that are transpiring on Earth at this moment are the decisions and negotiations and power struggles that will determine how this secret material will be revealed, so we are channeling this at a time when decisions are still being made. The energy of your planet is going through this consciousness shift, this frequency elevation, regardless of the decisions made on your planet.

You are faced with an inevitability of energetics. You can pray and fast and do many things, but you cannot stop the Sun from rising. You cannot do that with the consciousness you have. At this time in Earth's evolution, you cannot stop the shifts and changes that are coming. What you can do is remove from your mind that which is hateful, that which is unloving, and that which is of such a disparate frequency that it will cause conflict. As you come to understand what these differing frequencies mean to each other, you will know how to transform your inner world.

So if you are paying attention to your mass media and are frightened about the future because you believe all the stories about the reasons for the wars and the justifications for military spending, know that as these energies pick up and shift, they are moving very quickly. If you believe all the fearmongering and the structure of the world that it implies, then as these energies shift into higher and higher gears, you will be left behind.

As you read this book, you will, in fact, expand your consciousness, align more with truth, and raise your frequency. Ignorance is not bliss. Knowledge helps you understand what will become manifest on your planet over the next few years. We really encourage you to allow the discomfort of these growth pains. It is important that you grow as quickly as possible without scaring yourself too much and becoming imbalanced.

If you begin to feel a little anxious and you don't feel stable in your consciousness, put the book down for a little while, and allow your mind to digest some of this revolutionary information. You have been raised in a Judeo-Christian society, which teaches you that you are the center of the universe, that God has created you, that there is only one race, and that the history of your planet has been very short and completely devoid of intelligent life until you showed up. This is not so. You have a mind that is fundamentally flawed in the way that it looks at the world. This is not your fault, but it is your responsibility to heal it. It is your responsibility to change it, and it is your responsibility to act in accord with this new understanding.

If you hold a low frequency, know that Gaia's higher frequencies as she transforms into a fifth-dimensional being are going to be intolerable for the closed, limited, fearful, and judgmental mind. You must change your mind to join in this journey to higher frequencies.

## Exercises to Help You Shift

How does the Holocaust play into this? Well, as we have said ad nauseam, the manipulations by your society have caused you to develop a very fearful, materialistic opinion about this particular event. In fact, you have been trained to look at all events in this way because you have been kept away from the truth of your divine nature — the truth that you live multiple lives as a consciousness, exploring through experience. You have been kept ignorant of the tremendous number of extraterrestrial beings that have seeded and assisted your planet as well as the tremendous number of extraterrestrial beings who have manipulated, controlled, and devalued your planet. Really honor this process that you are going through. This is not just a book that you are reading, some made-up fairy story; this is a true revelation of material that your mind requires to join in this evolutionary journey of consciousness that your planet will go through.

As you explore your consciousness, you will immediately feel when an idea we introduce is counter to a belief you currently hold. Now, there is a certain act of faith in listening to us. Of course at any time, you can dismiss this teaching, saying "This is crazy! There are no such experiments, no such lies and deceptions. The world is as I see it, as I have been taught." You are free to make that decision. This is an area of free will. You are allowed to make any decision you wish, just as Hitler was allowed to make any decision he wished. But at this stage of the game, we want you to make a particular decision: We want you to study the lessons of *A Course in Miracles*.

Now, that book is challenging for many of you in the modern world. The language and the discipline required are challenging, but with the time constraints you are facing on you planet at this time, if you wish to join in this consciousness evolution revolution, then you must put in the effort to shift your consciousness. Remember, you have had your minds manipulated. Remember, you have been intentionally taught, with great repetition and force, many things that are not true because the beings who wanted to control you knew they had to do it that way.

The only way you can get human beings to do what you want in this realm of free will is to make them believe they must make that decision. If you convince humans that the wrong decision is the right decision, they are still using their free will. You have tricked them into using their creative minds, their cocreative power, to bring into being what you want. This is what the powers that be — the hierarchies that have ruled your planet — have done.

In doing the lessons of *A Course in Miracles*, you take back your mind and the innate, loving frequency that is your birthright. You are made for love, from love, and by love. You are a divine aspect of God mind naturally attuned to love, and that is why you suffer so on this planet. You suffer because your minds have been taught to hate, judge, attack, and kill.

This is why you are in so much pain. You think it is the state of the world out there, but it is not. The state of your mind is causing this suffering.

The series of 365 lessons will take you on a journey from ignorance to understanding. It will take you on a journey from conflict to peace. It will not enlighten you, but it will allow you to look at the world with a much clearer perception. It will direct your mind again and again from attack and judgment to love and from disturbance to peace, and at the end of the 365 lessons, your mind will go through a clarification process that begins your ascension journey. But because of the time constraints you face, it is imperative to discipline your consciousness because it has been poorly and hatefully trained and viciously manipulated. Be willing to transform it in a very focused and intentional way now so that you can catch up on some of the lost areas of frequency that should belong to you.

We are Ananda, and we are here to help reveal what is necessary for you to go on this ride with Gaia. We have not spoken about many of these things before, and we understand that those of you who are valued participants in these teachings and have read our books are surprised at some of the things we are saying, but we have had an intentional plan for revealing this information to you.

The books you have read and the transmissions you have listened to have been taking you further and further up the ladder to understanding this information. If you step on the ladder at a rung that is too high for your consciousness to deal with, you will not succeed at the transformation of mind that we are asking you to make. Do not feel that going back to one of the earlier books is failure. It is not; it is sanity. It is like trying to run a marathon when you have not trained. You must train your mind as you must train your body; otherwise, you will injure yourself. You will have anxiety attacks or even psychotic breaks. Do not pursue things for which you are not prepared.

So once again, we ask you to study *A Course in Miracles*. The lessons are the most powerful aspect of that book, and you can start those very easily and quickly without too much preparation. The information that we provide is enough to introduce you to the concepts of nonduality. That is what these teachings are based on, that there is only one energy, and it is love. You are either tuning in to it or blocking it. That is all that is happening here. You must figure out where you block the energy of love. You block it through judgment, hatred, and fear, and that is why these hierar-chical systems have been so successful: They have learned how to put you in those low-frequency states so that you seem to be separated from love, God, the benevolent force that creates all life, all growth, and all the won-derful things that this universe expresses throughout its many systems.

The Holocaust must be released. This is a difficult task for the mind that is deeply indoctrinated in the Western way, but we know we can help you get there. We know we can encourage you to grow and learn and push through those difficult barriers of confusion and concern.

The time is now; you have run out of options. The duty of the expand-ing mind is to step up its frequency as much as possible in the next year. That is our recommendation. We use the word "duty," which is not some-thing we throw around lightly. If you seek awakening, love, and harmoni-ous existence, then it is your duty to step up your vibration. Nobody else can do it for you. You cannot heal that which is chosen. If you choose war, fear, resentment, and unforgiveness, you will reap the energy of the seeds you sow not as punishment or retribution but as the reflection that this universe endlessly offers you.

# CHAPTER 14

# The Dark Secret Revealed

Your destiny as a planet is written in the decisions you make in this time frame. You have had many lessons come your way on your planet through repeated opportunities to choose love, fear, forgiveness, or hatred, and because of the structure of your society, you have chosen hatred and fear time and time again. That is what you have been taught to do.

Now we are here to rattle your cage and to tell you that the time for choice has come to an end. We are not trying to frighten you (your governments are doing that well enough), but it is time to choose love above all. Do it without equivocating, arguing, or saying, "Oh, but it takes a long time! I don't want to practice the lessons of *A Course in Miracles*. I'm too busy. I have children, I have a job, and I have a mortgage. I don't have the freedom and time to do this." If you don't do it, you will miss the train!

What does that mean? As your planet evolves, you must go with her. The fleas on a dog must go with the dog. They need the dog for survival. They live off the nutrition the dog gives them. In your strong ego consciousness, you act as if you have an independent life. Well, you don't. If you don't go along with the planet, you will die because you will not have the nutrition, support, and loving energy you need. You are not independent of your planet, but you have been trained to believe that you are.

You go to stores where food is sold in trays and boxes, and you think that is where food comes from. No, food is generated from within the body of Gaia, and she is not optional in your evolutionary journey. She is not an element of your evolutionary journey that you can dismiss at the level of consciousness you hold when you are deeply focused on the material. You can change your connection to Gaia as you raise your frequency, but those of you caught in this Western programming system cannot achieve those levels without effort. That is what we are here to teach you. Most of you want a story and do not want to know how to fix the problem. You want demonstrations and illustrations of what the story is. We will give you a story so that you can understand.

Hitler was born on this planet to provide a service. This is not what you are taught about him. He was brought to this planet to manifest the darkest dualistic system on your world. He chose that role for many reasons. Just as Judas chose the role of the betrayer of your beloved Jesus, so did Hitler choose his role, and it is difficult to choose the role of the bad guy.

Before you are born in a body, each of you chooses the role you will play based on your experiences, your beliefs, and your knowledge of reality. At times, you will choose to play the good guy. Sometimes you'll play the bad guy. This is one reason that judging others is such a dangerous choice. In your ignorance and forgetfulness, you might look at someone who has, from a very evolved spiritual place, decided to play the bad guy, and you condemn that person and hate that person and waste all of your creative energy focusing on his or her negativities or what you believe is his or her evil nature.

There is no true evil in this dualistic system you are in. There are actors who play good guys and actors who play bad guys to illustrate, experience, and generate events and materializations.

Hitler chose to be who he was. He chose to be born into that country at that time to generate an experience for that generation. That generation was decided on because it was the one that would really turn the tide one way or another in the final evolution of that stage of your society's growth. So the Second World War and all the negativities that rose from Russia and Germany and the United States were all dramatic experiences designed to wake up humanity. That is not how they have been portrayed. They have been portrayed as sins, demagogues, dictators, and murderers, but in truth, many beings came to the Earth plane at that time to cause trouble to get your attention.

Now the same thing is playing out in the United States. "The Donald," as you call this brash and outspoken president, is the same kind of catalyst that you can use for your growth or for further hateful reflections. When a very negative being comes into power, it prompts a desire for the positive in people. That is what the negative demonstration does, and that is exactly what Hitler was designing in his pre-incarnational question-and-answer period. That is what he and his guides and teachers decided to precipitate — a negative event that would force love to reign and humanity to step up and offer support and love to the Jewish people.

Of course, Hitler persecuted many other groups in that time and place, and the West turned a blind eye. The West allowed this horrific, seemingly evil person to kill many beings before it finally stepped in. There were opportunities well before the end of the war for other countries to step in to accept refugees and offer them homes and support, but that opportunity to love was not taken. The opportunity for war — followed by negative programming and taking on some of the least lovable aspects of that regime — was taken.

After the war, the United States very quietly took in many German scientists and soldiers and beings high in the ranks of the SS and the Nazi war machine. Their experimentations, scientific knowledge, communications, and sometimes even magical processes that were used to manifest some of the darkness were taken on board within the deepest, most secretive parts of the U.S. government. The superficial story is that the German war machine was bad and that everything they did was condemned by the United States, but that is not true. The deepest, darkest secrets of that society were taken into North American society, where they were used and abused and continue to flourish behind closed doors.

This sounds like blasphemy to most North Americans. They do not believe this or understand it. Extraterrestrial beings revealed technology to the Germans in that time and place, and the United States wanted it. The U.S. government wanted access to this technology and essentially made a bit of a bargain with the devil. Of course, there is no devil, but the United States decided to give the Germans a place to work, hide, and start over in exchange for some of the technologies and relationships that those technologies had elicited between the less-evolved, less-loving extraterrestrial contacts that you are really not aware of.

From a spiritual point of view, Hitler was motivated from the deepest parts of his higher self from a loving place. That is what always takes place on the Earth plane despite the fact that when you believe in death and victims and perpetrators, it does not look that way. Every time somebody is manifested on the Earth plane, even in darkness, that person gives you the opportunity to respond with love and light, but that is not what happened.

## The Battle between Love and Fear

The energy of darkness entered the heart of America and the Western world, and it was used unapologetically in those realms. Dark, secret space and mind-training programs were taken over by the United States of America, and those unusual sources of information and unloving practices were used to manipulate and control, just as the German people were manipulated and controlled through propaganda, mind training, and social and genetic engineering.

Those things, then, became imported in the West, and that is why the country of Israel was created. It was created to play a role in this deception. It was created to be able to justify all kinds of atrocities, all kinds of warmongering, and all kinds of seemingly defensive postures to "prevent" the Holocaust from happening again. But those beings who developed that country, that society, in the Middle East knew exactly what they were doing. They wanted access to areas of the world that they could not justify otherwise, so they created a place where the supposedly victimized Jewish people of the world could go. They painted a very pretty picture on what was, energetically speaking, a very unloving structure.

That is what you have seen over the past few decades on your planet. You have seen the unloving nature of that country's fundamental reason for being. Its fundamental reason for being is not to provide a safe home for the Jewish people; it is to reinforce the victim-perpetrator mentality so that war crimes can be committed. That is what that country does. It is a blatant physical and geopolitical statement that Jewish people will never be safe. They are forever persecuted and victimized; therefore, war is justified. Defense and attack are justified.

So instead of the world rising up after the Holocaust and saying, "That will never happen again! We must give loving support to Jewish people in our homes and in our countries. We must give them places to live," the anti-Semitic nature of the paradigm that was playing out created a giant ghetto with an underlying agenda to justify warmongering and, of course, the possession of these sacred vortexes and spaces that have been used by humanity for both good and bad. They have even been abused by humanity at times. The battle in the Middle East is over the control of these ancient and powerful gateways into other parts of the universe.

We know this is considered blasphemy in your world, and we know these kinds of stories are considered anti-Semitic. That has become a sacred cow of your society because of the stories that have been told about the Holocaust. However, the face of innocence that is painted on the United States as it relates to the Holocaust, post-war Germany, and Israel is fictitious and insincere. It is a face of deception, and the true power structures of your society have been playing very cruel games for a long time with all of you.

We are here to open Pandora's box, and yes, it is Pandora's box. Once you begin to look at the truth with an open and honest gaze, you will see the games, the abuses, and the unloving structures that are attempting to maintain control of that part of the world.

## Side with Love

The mechanisms of control will begin to waiver and fail, and that is why this is such important information for you to hold at this time. This story is not going to be short-lived. It is going to take many years to undo that which has been done to your minds, that which has been done to the Middle East, and that which has been done to the poor victims of these horrific war crimes. It is going to take many years to heal these wounds and to rectify the damage that has been done in that part of the world. Until you hear the truth, you will not be willing to make the internal shifts and changes that you need to make so that you can create a different future.

This future is not going to look like the past 100 years or so of your planet. The past 100 years or so have seen darkness rule. The past 100 years have seen an emergence of a New Age philosophy that increased spirituality and focus on love and forgiveness, but you have also seen an amplification of the wars, hatred, separation, and psychological manipulation.

What is being reached now and will take place in the next few years is the battle between love and fear.

We are on the side of love. We are revealing the truth so that you, in your powerful ability to side with love or fear, have enough information to decide to side with love. Not until you all side with love, can this world change because it is a collective consciousness. You all contribute to the light or the dark. Every decision you make, every word you say, and every action you participate in is either loving or fearful. It is either expansive or retracted. It is either hostile or kind. The choices are only between those two things.

We are here to reveal the dark underbelly of your society so that you can say, "Enough is enough! I am no longer buying into the fictitious stories that these governments tell us. I am going to side with love, which means that the bombing, war, separation, isolation, and pain must stop. I will do whatever I can (in my mind first) to side with humanity and equality and kindness, and as I change my mind, I will act in accord with those beliefs so that everyone around me knows war is not okay, no matter the justification!"

There is no justification for war. Going into any country to drop bombs that kill children and to maim and distort and destroy cultures is not justifiable under any circumstances. We ask you to cease using the Holocaust as your justification for going into the Middle East and destroying cultures and people's homes, hearts, and families.

# CHAPTER 15

# Modern Methods of Frequency Manipulation

Your destiny is being determined right now, so if you are reading this for recreation, you are not taking the wisest approach. Recreation time is over on your planet. Your recreations have been used to manipulate and control you just as many of your systems have been used to manipulate and control you.

Entertainment is an addiction in your society. The entertainment industry is hypnotic and control focused, and it lulls you into lowering your frequency in many ways. For example, many of you see the sexual revolution as something that was very beneficial to humanity. You can have sex with whomever you want to, wear whatever clothes you want to, and be the sexual being that you know you are. The way sexuality is marketed in your Western society is detrimental to your spiritual growth. We are speaking specifically about the advertising, movies, and pornography of Western society.

Many of you are concerned about puritanical beliefs and celibacy because spirituality has been deemed as holy and sex deemed as unholy. This is not what we are saying at all. Our opinion of sexual energy that is very high frequency and loving in nature is very accepting, and we value that energy. However, Your entertainment systems are being intentionally flooded with lower forms of sexual energy. When the human body is marketed in this way (it is increasingly happening to men but is predominantly happening to women), you are confused. You think you can dress any way you want because you have become liberated somehow. This is a continuation of the patriarchal society. You have not become liberated energetically. When we see young girls wearing very short skirts or teenage girls wearing very low necklines to display themselves as products for consumption, they are energetically suffering terribly, and they are energetically being consumed as products.

We speak about the energetics of these systems because you are ignorant of them. You have been intentionally indoctrinated in the material and physical world to keep your attention away from your feelings, your emotions, those little warning bells your intuition gives you from the unseen world of energy. You have been trained not to pay attention to this. In fact, you will override your own energy systems with drugs and alcohol and many other devices because you have been told that your feelings are worthless and your emotions are troublesome and not worthy of any respect. Only the unfeeling intellect is of value. This is a deep indoctrination in your society, and it allows your incredible power to be siphoned from your society.

## The Manipulation of Sexual Energy

The beings long in charge of your society have used fear, manipulation, and control from the beginning. They understand that to thwart the tremendous power of the connected individual, they had to perpetuate separation, fear, and limitation, and that is exactly what they have done, starting in the Middle East at the beginning of what you think of as your modern history with controls, taxation, war, and manipulation. It was initiated about 3,500 years ago with contact from highly intelligent extraterrestrial beings with nefarious intentions. This is where your world began to lose direction and its ability to discern clearly. These beings were masters of energy and mind control, things you were not experienced with. Consequently, you were trained away from self-awareness. Your churches manipulated you to hand over your decision-making processes to them.

Breaking out of regimentation is what you will do with your energies because you are freedom-seeking, creative, and loving beings. You will seek freedom to express new ideas, to love each other, and to make love with each other. That is your natural state.

When you look back on your society, you can see that there have been prescriptions, prohibitions, and limiting — and at times, lethal — methods to stop you from playing in the woods, with each other, and with yourselves for thousands of years. These have been deeply ingrained in the collective consciousness, and that is affecting your modern society, believe it or not. Many of you feel shame about sexuality, yet in this modern world, you receive messages to flaunt and expose your body and to give it up for entertainment purposes. This is a low form of sexual energy, and it is one of the biggest areas in which you are losing your power, your force.

If you go to the inner, energetic world of the modern Western woman, you will find a great deal of shame and self-loathing have been indoctrinated and engendered in her psyche, manipulated through modern movies and television programs, including (of course) pornography. These are intentionally used to keep sexual energies at the lowest frequencies possible, which is almost an animalistic level, and that is why so many of you have difficulty in intimately relating to each other. It is why so many of you have been raped or abused by trusted adults when you were children. It is why there have been so many abuses within the church. They know exactly how powerful sexual energy is as an energetic system.

When you raise sexual energy to the realms of love, it maintains its power and turns into the most benevolent creative force there is. Of course, the making of a new vehicle for a nonphysical being to enter for a new physical experience is one of the great gifts of your world. You will notice that people are having difficulty getting pregnant or are postponing having children because children are inconvenient, messy, and noisy. People seem to prefer their nice apartments and cell phones. These are ways that your innate power is siphoned off or kept low.

## You Always Have a Choice

As you go through your day, it is very important to ask yourself whether you are marketing yourself as a product. Are you getting ready to sell yourself when you go out the door? We are not judging you for this; we are merely trying to reveal the multifaceted domination that has been at work in your world. What does this have to do with the Holocaust? Well the Holocaust was the ultimate play from Spirit's side to wake you as you enter the last phases of your third-dimensional journey with Gaia.

She is advancing to another level, and from Spirit's point of view, you were given the opportunity to grow exponentially through the correct interpretation of the Holocaust, all those beings who volunteered to come in as victims and all those perpetrators who came in to play the bad guys to demonstrate these principles.

This collective creation could have been a positive thing if it had been interpreted properly: the cruelty and horribleness of it had been witnessed, and love had arisen from that darkness, which is always the possibility. You can always choose to forgive, love, and experience unity rather than separation. This is always the case. If you are raped or a drunk driver kills someone in your family, you have the opportunity to continue separation through hatred and vengeance or to forgive, reconcile, and in the end, love. That is what you always face on this planet. It will not go away until you choose love time after time.

The intention behind the Holocaust was to get you to choose love. It was a big, loud demonstration of darkness to elicit a big demonstration of light and love in response. But because the people in charge understood how the mind and feelings work, they manipulated you into holding the frequency of hatred and fear decade after decade so that they could maintain their power and control you. They have been using many mind-control techniques through forms of entertainment to maintain the low-frequency aspects of your emotional guidance system, keeping them in play so that you are fearful, self-loathing, and obsessed with your body.

As long as you are obsessed with your body — you believe your value lies in your body, you attack your body, or you worship your body — you will witness something like the Holocaust and have no choice but to condemn the perpetrators. As long as you believe your body is who you are, you will believe the victims were their bodies. They were eternal spiritual beings who made choices just as you are an eternal spiritual being making choices now. But as long as you stay in a body-worshiping, materialistic, consumer vibration, you will fear, believe in, and worship death. That is the nature of the ego. It loves to fight, it loves to war, it loves to kill, and it loves to separate, and the entertainment industry keeps you in that state. So when we repeatedly tell you to turn off your televisions and be careful about the movies you watch, we are not doing it to be naysayers or party poopers (as you say it). We are telling you that those systems of mass management are the most lethal drug you consume.

Violent sports such as ice hockey, football, rugby, boxing, and mixed martial arts are also like drugs. These keep the masculine down. Women are kept in the lower frequencies by the marketing of their bodies, the consumption of their bodies as products, which keeps them feeling very vulnerable and concerned about their value — they are not attractive enough or are too fat or whatever mechanism is used — and men are indoctrinated in war through games of battle. The collective energy produced by spectators of a fight, for instance, is very low. If you could see the frequency of the beings who feed off your anger and rage, you would be horrified.

Just as you can be healed by love and the higher frequencies of Spirit, as demonstrated in beings such as Jesus, you can be infected and depleted by lower-frequency consciousnesses you cannot see or detect through your dumbed-down systems of sight and sound. You have been told to trust only these limited physical structures. "Don't trust your feelings, your dreams, or your intuition," you are told. These are the mechanisms of control, fear, and darkness that your society is utterly infected with.

Young men are conditioned to go into battle on the sports field. You are conditioned to be aggressive through cartoons of sword-wielding knights battling each other in a contest of good versus evil. By the time boys are five or six years old, they have been deeply indoctrinated for war and violence, and it continues on and on and on.

These are some of the manipulations you experience in this society, but we want you to know that they all rely on you to participate. This is a freewill zone. You must choose what you put in your mind, body, and heart. You choose what you consume. You are the decision maker. This never changes, and this is the law we want to draw your attention to: You always have a choice.

You can choose whether to buy a piece of meat or a beautiful, fresh piece of fruit. You can choose whether to plug into television or to go for a walk. Nobody is forcing you, but the hierarchical structures and controlling mechanisms of your society know how to push your buttons because they invented those buttons. From the time you were little, they have trained you to want, and what you want is what they want.

Now is the time to deactivate these buttons, but you must decide to do it. "Yes, I know. My father watched Sunday afternoon football with me all the time, but it is an aggressive and violent game, and its energy is relentless." How many football games do you need to watch before you realize you are participating in a violent activity? You might not be throwing the punches or hurling your body at someone else's, but you consume that frequency.

The frequencies you consume, the ones you hold in your mind through your thoughts and beliefs and the things you say to yourself, are the frequencies that manifest your world and your body. Many of you who are sick or aging in unpleasant ways are suffering the consequences of holding these very low frequencies for a long time. Yes, all these things can be reversed, but you must realize what is being done so that you can make a different choice.

You have been brainwashed. You have been told "this" is good or patriotic. It is the way to do things and the way to look, so you might feel very uncomfortable when you step away from these prescriptions and control mechanisms.

## Turn Off the Violence in Your Mind

These systems will break down. Before they do, you would be well served to remove yourself from them consciously (with guidance on a spiritual path), knowing that you are doing something that benefits not only yourselves and your family but also all of humanity.

You will benefit every time you walk away from violence. You will benefit every time you decide that your body is not who you are — that you are not a product — and that your value lies not in your beauty or your muscles but in your heart, your soul, your creativity, and your ability to love and care for yourselves, your children, your families, and your communities. These are the reasons you are here. You are not here to attain the American dream or the Western dream. That is an illusion, and it contributes, believe it or not, to the warmongering in the Middle East. It allows you, in your war-trained and violence-saturated minds, to look at the atrocities there and say, "Oh well, what can I do?"

You can do something: Turn off the violence in your minds. Turn off the violence in your children's lives. Do not do to them what has been done to you. Do not condemn them to the same violence you have witnessed. It is not a mistake; it is a planned and intelligently executed mind-control program that is coming to a very violent end because of the sheer number of you who have participated in the energetic system of hatred, fear, judgment, and war.

We do not judge you for these energy systems or for watching these movies and playing these games, but we warn you that your time is up. The jig is up. If you want a high-frequency experience — a loving family and a loving life full of health, abundance, joy, creativity, and eager anticipation for a good future — you must step away from these programs, dear ones. You must unplug them now.

You must pray for your enemies, and you must insist on peaceful resolutions. Do the work in your mind first because that is where everything generates. These hierarchies know that. They have infiltrated your mind and implanted programs and fictitious ideas and beliefs.

Get back to nature and natural things. Clothe yourself with comfortable and respectable and good-feeling garments that honor your beauty, your strength, and your spiritual nature. These sound like old-fashioned ideas, but they are not. They are truthful concepts that have been eradicated from your collective consciousness by the systematic and relentless pursuit of violence, war, and energy-siphoning sexual predators. They consume you.

You are powerful beings, and that is why so much effort has been put into harvesting your energy, your focus, your beliefs, and your cocreative abilities. Do not think of yourselves as weak because this happened. These systems were strategically designed and implemented because you are strong.

Take back your power. Get out in nature. Turn these systems off. Get into your creativity, your communities, and your conversations with each other. Reach out loving hands to each other so that you have strong communities when these precarious structures begin to topple. They will topple because Earth has made a decision. She is moving up in frequency, and everything that is not high frequency will not travel with her, so all of these unloving and hateful systems are going to begin to teeter. You can see it happening now. Be sure to prepare for these transitional times.

# CHAPTER 16

# Implement Your Spiritual Reconditioning Program

These conversations are designed to open your consciousness, not to upset you. However, opening the consciousness can be distressing to a mind that is not used to expansion. This is where most of you are in your development: You are constantly told to stay at your job, make your mortgage payment, do things that you do not want to do, and believe messages from mainstream media that are not true even though you feel in your heart that something is up. You look at the world and know that the beings in charge are not doing a very good job, but your training tells you to keep doing what you are doing. These transmissions will upset that apple cart.

We want you to know the symptoms of an expanding mind so that you do not feel fear, because that is what you have been trained to interpret conflict as. You have been trained to interpret conflict as fear when, in fact, conflict is the mind just trying to sort out information.

We are adding very different information to your body-mind complex. It is coming from many sources. We are not one being; we are many beings. Some of us are involved in the orchestration of the transformation of your world, so you might consider us extraterrestrials. Only high-frequency extraterrestrial beings can transmit through this particular voice structure. Beings who have great concern for your planet are bringing information through this channel that will help you make decisions and interpret some of the erroneous information you will witness over the next few years. We want you to react appropriately to information. That means when a being of high frequency instructs you on how to alleviate fear, follow those prescriptions.

So you might feel agitation and confusion from these words because this information doesn't seem appropriate given the beliefs you hold about spirituality. Many of you have read our books and have taken an elevating path of frequency. The subjects covered in previous texts are foundational belief structures that allow you to interpret this information correctly. Each was brought through in a time and place to help create building blocks with which you can construct a new society.

Some of these building blocks are very important, such as learning about sexual energy and the history of the Christian church. If you haven't questioned those beliefs or expanded your views on those subjects, this subject will be much more difficult for you to handle. You would not jump from the first level to the sixth level in a fitness program. You know you would be out of breath, you wouldn't enjoy it, you wouldn't understand, your muscles wouldn't be strong enough, and so on. This is similar. You are on a spiritual reconditioning plan, and it is very important that you behave according to that plan.

Beings contained within our consciousness group are currently residing in your three-dimensional space-time reality, and you would consider them to be extraterrestrials. They have physical bodies, they reside within your time frame, they visit your planet, and they observe your governments' and your society's workings. They are distressed, to say the least, about what is happening on your planet. They offer information through this guardian to assist in realigning your mind with a frequency that will help your society grow and evolve.

## Take Your Foot Off the Brake

When we commune with you, we act as gatekeepers. This channel is very open to multifaceted, multidimensional communications, and she has a gatekeeper who keeps her safe and the information at a high level, a level that will assist humanity. That is what we are doing with this information about the Middle East, Israel, and the founding belief structures that are causing the decision-making processes you are witnessing. The hierarchical structures have intentionally hidden from you the power of the communal mind and of your cocreative abilities. The more people align with love and this knowledge, the quicker changes can take place in your society. The more people plug into television and medicate themselves through various systems, the longer the transformation will take.

This transformation of consciousness is taking place on your planet. It is not optional. But the collective energy of unconscious beings is like a foot on the brake. The high-frequency shifts coming to your planet are like a foot on the gas. Those of you who drive understand what happens when you put your foot on the brakes and the gas at the same time: Your wheels spin, and you burn out the tires, the brakes, and eventually the engine. This will not be a smooth and easygoing transition if you take that approach. We are attempting to get you to take your foot off the brake. What is the brake? The brake is judgment, separation, fear, and nationalism.

Now, we know that many of you see the agenda of globalists, and you fear the road they are taking you down. This is an appropriate reaction, but we don't want to keep you in fear. You don't want to stay in fear. Remember, that is one thing that keeps your foot on the brake. We want you to say, "Globalism, in its current form, is not beneficial to this unique experience on this Earth plane. Local governments need to understand us. We need decision-making processes close to home that reflect our society and our needs and desires within our communities." You do not need to fear globalism. You need to say, "That is not what we need," and then put all your creative energies toward what you want, which is a strong local community and a sane and humanitarian local government that develops projects that support humanity that are compassionate, kind, organic, and helpful.

Do not remain in an antiglobalist mindset. Merely observe what it is doing — destroying your planet — and then focus your powerful creative energies toward local action inspired by a desire for a sane and loving community. This is how you will be able to manifest that which you want.

## You Are in This Together

Disclosure is coming your way. Many secret government programs, actions, monitoring systems, and manipulation systems will come into the daylight. However, a lot of healing will be needed as you discover these deceptive programs. If you have not had any training in loving mind control (such as being able to focus your mind wherever you wish, not allowing somebody else to direct your focus), then these revelations will be very distressing because you will feel victimized, you will feel fear, you will feel intense judgment, and you will feel hatred and even a desire for retribution. But if you have aligned your mind with love and have accepted that this is a cocreative process, then you will not feel victimized.

The deceptions were designed to get you to make decisions that support negative and unhealthy systems. You will realize that very clever beings played a game to get you to make the moves they wanted you to make. In fact, you were using your free will. You decided to buy a gas-guzzling car because you fell for the commercials. These are ways that manipulation is used. However, you do not want to remain angry or resentful about these things. Take that energy of desiring fairness, health, and peace, and apply it where you are. Make decisions that come from a place of love, a place of kindness, and a place of awareness about what is happening. This is what will unfold in your society over the next few years, and if you do not have your thoughts and emotions clarified and aligned correctly, there will be a great deal of fear. There might even be violent outbursts and rioting in the streets because people will be angry and feel justified in retribution. You are never justified in attacking anybody.

This is a world of oneness. This is a consciousness that is unified, so when you attack a brother, you attack yourself, and you will suffer for it. The only solutions for the separation, deception, and lies in your society are honesty, openness, connectedness, community, and love. No matter what information you receive, your response must be so; otherwise you will join in the frequency of hatred and war, and that will continue to thrive on your planet.

These higher-frequency beings using this channel want you to know the alignment with love is not an airy-fairy spiritual wish list. It is what you must do to manifest the physical experiences and the healing you want to see in the world. They are assisting, but they are not allowed to guide you physically. They can only point you in the direction that they want you to go and ask you to use your free will to make new decisions.

As your guides and counselors, we are telling you that you are not free to make loving decisions if your mind is still contaminated with old stories about the Holocaust and the righteousness of the United States and its relationship with Israel. These are lies that have been used to manipulate that part of the world, and until you are willing to change your mind about what is going on there, you will remain trained in that thought paradigm of retribution, attack, war, and destruction. That is what you are seeing.

You are seeing people who believe bombing and interfering in sovereign countries are the best courses of action. You see this in many places in that part of the world, and it counts on your training to keep you quiet and passive and feeling victimized. We are here to tell you that victimization is not your salvation; that is in taking back your mind, learning to interpret your emotional guidance system, and listening to the voices of higher-frequency beings who can see your future in several forms.

One potential reality is that you don't choose love, so you continue to attack and judge and live in fear. That would lead to a militarized global system that is completely oppressive and in which you lose your freedom. There are other future timelines you can jump to, but this requires taking back your personal creative power and understanding that the more beings who step into that powerful place of loving focus, gentle action, and considerate words — the more of you who get together in that frequency — the better your frequency will be.

Creation is a natural aspect of you. You have all been created in the image of God. You are able to infinitely create whatever it is that you focus on. If you keep focusing on the Holocaust and its potential re-creation, it is bound to manifest. Essentially, it already has. But you are powerful as a group and individually. When aligned with love, one person can transform the world, so imagine what you can do together.

Start looking at your brothers and sisters in your community as beings who reflect you. When you walk down the street, don't look at others as others. Instead, smile and say, "Everything I give to you, I give to me. This is a mutually beneficial relationship." Envision your heart opening, and feel where your fears and defenses lie. Make note of these. "Ah, whenever I think about opening my heart to my husband (or wife), I feel defensive. I feel as if I am going to be hurt. Let me contemplate that subject. Let me be healed of that limiting thought and belief." If you have not yet started the lessons of *A Course in Miracles*, we advise you to do that to help you.

Only in transforming your consciousness will you see a change in the world. The powers that be have told you that you have no power and you must vote them in. All you have is one tiny vote that really doesn't count for much. Their story is the lie, and our story is the truth. Take back your power, but first take back your mind. You must learn to interpret your emotions correctly, and you must act the way you would like others to act toward you.

# PART 2

# The Galactic Federation Supports Earth's Evolution

*Extraterrestrials Speak*

# CHAPTER 17

# Spirituality Is Universal

*Ananda and the Andromedan Galactic Council*

e are Ananda. Your journey with us is very important at this stage of your planet's evolution, and we want you to know that you have been called to action. You have been called to set aside your old beliefs and step into a new paradigm with us. While this might seem like some grand assignment that you feel you are not qualified to do, many of you have come here at this time to assist your planet through this tremendous evolutionary leap that is being assisted in its implementation from nonphysical beings such as us, and extraterrestrial beings of high frequency who are communicating through this channel.

Now we are happy to share a transmission from one of the extraterrestrial beings who are assigned with your transformative education. These extraterrestrials are known as the Andromedan Galactic Council, and they are particularly loving beings. They are connected to a group of disparate extraterrestrial associations that come together to assist humanity in transformation. The following pages contain direct communication from the Andromedan Galactic Council head. The being will introduce itself, and we will stand by to guard the frequency of this being and to make sure there are no interruptions, no lower frequency transmissions, and no conflicts of thought, word, or deed.

[Note: The following words were spoken in a very different voice from Ananda's, and they had a strong, direct energy behind them.]

✳   ✳   ✳

Your connection to us is very special. We are the Andromedan Council associated with the Galactic Federation. We are here to bring into your dimension the information you need so that you can assist us in assisting you.

We are here to help raise your frequency out of egoic consciousness, out of war, and out of the indoctrinated fear that you have been drawn into over millennia. We are here to help you understand that you are not alone in the universe. We wait outside your common view to help you. You are not ready to see us. You are not ready yet to speak in person with us and to view our physical forms, but you are ready to hear our message, which is one of love, compassion, and education. We come with a great phalanx of specialists, theorists, engineers, healers, and teachers. We come with many plants and animals to help clarify your planet. It has been taken into a dark age through the negative programming that is constantly beamed into your bodies and your hearts and your minds.

## About the Andromedan Council

We want you to know that you have made a sound choice. The Andromedan Council associated with the Galactic Federation consists of loving beings who have your society's growth and healing as their purpose. We have come here for that purpose. There are no conflicts in our hearts or in our minds. We have overcome war, we have overcome sickness, and we have overcome a dependency on solid, three-dimensional matter that you believe is the only world you can live on. We can travel through time, we can travel through mind, and we can travel through our hearts into your hearts. We have a tremendous ability to communicate with you when you open your minds to this idea.

Societal teachers have given you a narrow view of spirituality, your world, and your universe that has kept you very small. You must understand that spirituality goes far beyond the small human community on your planet. Spirituality permeates the universe. It permeates this galaxy with millions and millions of planets that can and do support life in forms that you would respect and understand as humanoid.

We are humanoid in form. If you saw us, you would recognize our body shapes as similar to yours, but we have physical differences. Our hair is blonder and straighter, and our eyes are larger. We are taller, slenderer, and paler than you, but we would not seem so unusual on your Earth plane. We would be considered startlingly good-looking, if you want to have a smile about it. We would be considered model-like. You might wonder, "Are they from Scandinavia? Where do these elegant and sophisticated people come from?"

We are here as your friends to bring developing society the information you need. What we bring is what you have lost. Your society was much more evolved several thousand years ago, but it has plummeted into darkness because of the teachings the rulers of your world have forced down your throats, so to speak.

We associate with high-frequency nonphysical and physical beings. There are beings on your planet who know of our existence and have been communicating with us much in the same form as this being is communicating with us. She allows her mind to open and take in the transmissions we bring forth. We teach her often in her sleep, and we reveal some of the physical encounters she will have over the next few years in her dreams so that her consciousness can get used to that idea. That is something we will do with all of you when you are willing to open your minds to conscious contact with high-frequency and loving extraterrestrial beings who want to assist your planet out of the darkness it has plummeted into.

The Andromedan Council is a collection of many societies in the Andromedan galaxy. We travel through time and space to come to you because we care for you as part of our family of light. We are your ancestors. We have come to your planet many times, and we have brought fruits of our society to your society, but it has been hard to plant those seeds because your minds have been contaminated with fear and judgment.

Now the evolution of your society is taking place with much help from nonphysical beings and from highly evolved extraterrestrial beings who can wield power and influence that prevent further destruction of your minds and your hearts. The turning point in your society has come, and you must choose the light. You must choose love, and you must choose to take back your consciousness, offering it only to beings who care about your health and well-being as we do.

## A Healing Phase Is Required

Those who are suspicious of our message might say, "How do we know you are good? How do we know that you are kind and that you have our best interests at heart?" We say, how do you know your leaders have these things in their hearts — your health, your wealth, your well-being? Look around you. See the consequences of the decisions they make. You give them your life's blood: your taxes and your hard labor. You put your money in their banks, and you see that they are not looking after you very well, but you continue to comply with their demands and their wishes and their words. You put your lives and your children's lives into the arms and hands of beings who do not care for you.

We care for you greatly. We have traveled far, and we are here, in our ships, waiting for the shift in consciousness that is required for us to present ourselves in physical form. We must wait for all of you to become willing to interact with us in a loving way. It must first take place in your minds. You must decide that we are your friends. You must decide that we are here to communicate only good things to you. We bring forth information from many specialists and many specialties — engineering, medicine, bioengineering, biology, education, and philosophy. All kinds of specialists are coming to help your planet and you heal and understand yourselves better. You have been taught so many things that are incorrect that you need a healing phase in your society's development. You need to undo the damage, the trauma, that has been done.

Those who have gone to war and killed other beings must be healed of posttraumatic stress symptoms. Those who have had their energy systems shut down by religious doctrines must have those energy systems enlivened and awakened again. Those who have had their minds filled with hatred and fear must have those thoughts and ideas clarified and cleansed from within their consciousnesses. All these things must take place within rather than without. We offer those services to you, but you must understand your need for them. We cannot force them on you. You must come to the understanding within your consciousnesses, your hearts, and your feeling bodies.

You must see the chaos that is erupting on your planet, the lies and distortions that are being spread, the confusion and agitation that are arising, and the desertification of your planet's surface. Earth is struggling with oil, gas, and mineral extraction and gasoline consumption. These things are destroying your atmosphere, and you have a ticking time bomb on your hands. That is why we have come at this time — not to frighten you or to force you into anything, but to ask you to look honestly at the state you have taken yourselves to through deception, fear, and confusion.

The teachers in your world made you choose the wrong thing. They made you choose what they wanted you to choose, and now your free will must be returned to you in full awareness. You must understand that you are the decider. You are the one to pick what you will support, what you will allow into your consciousness, what you will love, and what you will hate. We are here, as a federation of highly evolved beings, to help your rehabilitation. We are here to ask you to entertain the idea that there are beings off your planet who care for you more than those who rule your planet. Our purpose is to plant this seed.

If you feel fear when we communicate in this way, you are not ready to entertain us in your consciousness, so let it go. Focus on loving yourself and your planet. Love the birds and the flowers and the animals you see trying to survive this holocaust of your earthly plane. If you are excited about this communication and you wish to have further connection with us, continue reading. Entertain the idea that we are your friends and that communication in your dream state and in your meditations will take place. We will do that with and for you.

We do not come here to scare you. We do not come here to force you or to intimidate you in any way. We only come here to hold your hands as you step out of the mire of fear and death and destruction that the rulers on your planet have taken you into. They are jumping like rats off a sinking ship, and they are even less caring for your well-being, so make sure that you really think about what we are saying. The sooner you change your minds and ask for help, the sooner we can help you.

## You Must Help Earth Heal

The world cannot be impinged on. We cannot force ourselves on you. The rulers of your planet did not force themselves on you; they intimidated you into supporting them. We ask with love in our hearts for you to turn to love instead of submitting to the fear they have used to destroy your minds, your hearts, and your environment. Your beautiful Earth can be saved if we bring all our powers to bear on her healing. That means you must bring all your cocreative energies to bear on her healing as well, and you must step away from the darkness. You must turn away from the old indoctrinations and open your hearts and minds to love. That is what these higher beings ask you to do now. They ask you to step away from the low-frequency indoctrinations of your society, look to the stars, call to us, and ask for our help.

We can help you if you invite us, but we cannot help you if you keep your sight on the ground in fear and smallness and supplication to the rulers of your world. We are the Andromedan Council associated with the Galactic Federation. We wish you well and ask you to continue reading.

There is going to be a great deal of excitement for those interested in extraterrestrial contact, and there will be fear in those who have limited their spiritual practice to the Earth plane. Know that that is not the only place that the being you call God plays. God plays in all universes, all galaxies, all planets, and all solar systems, and you are but a speck in a sea of multiplicities of specks expressing themselves.

You are a divine aspect of God mind expressing itself, but it has forgotten how grand God's mind is, and there are many of us out here who share the same experience of spirituality, the same experience of holiness, and the same experience of love that you do.

# CHAPTER 18

# The Call for Assistance

*The Andromedan Council*

We are the Andromedan Council associated with the Galactic Federation, and we come together from a hodgepodge of societies in our galaxy. We work together to bring peace and love and development to struggling societies.

Your society has had a very difficult time of it for a very long time because of negative and confusing influences that have been wielding power over you for millennia. Why is change happening now? The universe is a creation of the consciousness of that which you call God, divine in all its aspects, but there is a forgetting process that happens as each flame of consciousness is brought into physical being. You are each considered a small spark of the great fire you call God, and in that small spark is the same power as the whole of that creative force. A lit match holds the same qualities as a bonfire, and a bonfire holds the same qualities as a forest fire. Each one is unique and powerful in its own abilities. You are all like that. We are all like that. Each consciousness form brings into being its own version of that creative force.

When you are born in a physical incarnation on your planet, many things happen to you. First, you go through a forgetting process. That is part of the design. Part of the design is that you have a unique experience in each incarnation with a fresh opportunity to create new ideas, new experiences, and new opportunities. If you came into this incarnation with conscious knowledge of all other incarnations you have had, your experience would be too contaminated. You wouldn't have that fresh moment of striking the match and starting something new. So for the benefit of this new creation, you are given the gift of amnesia, and in that gift, you get a fresh start. However, in your society's conditioning process, that fresh start has a wet blanket thrown on it the second you are born in families that prefer fear, dysfunction, or violence to love. This is an ever-evolving confusion. You have been fed layer upon layer of confusion. Societies reach a point where lies outweigh truth, imprisonment outweighs opportunity, and restriction outweighs creativity. Your society has reached that point.

In this universe, when a society becomes oppressed or distorted to such a degree that it cannot create clearly anymore, a call goes out from those who are suffering on that plane. Those on your planet who suffer have sent a call for assistance that has been loud for the past several centuries, and it is getting louder. It is a voluntary call. It cannot be done for you or tricked out of you. It must be an honest call from deep within your consciousness that says, "I am not happy here. I am confused and in pain here, and I need help. I accept help from wherever it will come."

When this call goes up from a consciousness, we hear it. We are highly evolved telepathic beings who have great concern for your society. We have been watching your planet go through its devolution. We have been watching your planet go through its dark night of the soul. That is what the past thousand or so years have been for your planet.

Most of you look back on your history and wonder at the violence. You wonder at the horror and the numerous holocausts that have taken place on the surface of this most beautiful gem in the universe, the planet Earth. You wonder, "How can humans keep choosing negativity? How can humans keep choosing poverty and to kill each other in war after senseless war?" You are trained in it. You are taught about it, and you are separated from your true nature. You are deceived, and you are manipulated. As we said, there is a point in any society's development when pain outweighs joy, and your society has been there long enough. Now through this New Age expanding-consciousness movement, there are enough of you who have put out the call for assistance. You have said, "I cannot do this any longer!" You have said, "There must be a better way."

## Light Will Win

Your society is deeply involved in trading political associations and military operations with many antagonistic extraterrestrial forces. The messages and the images you are fed through your mass media are not accurate. You have been deceived more than you will ever know. There are thousands and thousands of interactions with extraterrestrial beings on your planet. Some are made through telecommunications systems to discuss deals and operations. Some are made in person. Some are made out in space, in what you would consider colonies where humanity has extended itself and has relationships with extraterrestrial beings.

Most extraterrestrial beings associated with your military-industrial complex and your earthbound governments are less than evolved. They have been playing on the chessboard of Earth's political realm for a long time, maneuvering, shifting, manipulating, controlling, terrorizing, and doing many other things. The dark side of humanity has joined in this game and participated in many trades, business deals, and warmongering thoughts and ideas. This is why you see your planet slipping slowly into oblivion, and you wonder why the powers that rule your world do not do something to stop it. Well, the powers that rule your world from behind the scenes are not human. They have not been human, so they do not care for humanity. That is why your world looks so insane. That is why your world looks (and is) so dangerous for humans: The powers that be and the rulers that rule their minds are not the same as you. They are not made from love, by love, and for love; they play on the dark side of the relativity game.

There is always a dualistic game between the light and the dark, but the light will always win because, in the end, the purpose of creation is to experience light and dark relativity and to find out how everything feels so that you can choose the one closest to love. It is like returning Home.

When young adults leave home, they don't want to be in their parents' presence anymore. They don't want to be at home anymore. They choose to take off into the wild blue yonder — head for the mountains or to foreign countries to find themselves and to have new experiences. But a time comes when they want to go home. A time comes when they realize that all these experiences lose their appeal, and that is when they turn around and take the long trek back to their hearts. The journey is the same for all beings in this universe. Some get lost on that trek away from home and become so confused that they forget they have a home. That is what happened to many of the higher-echelon humans on your plane at this time. They have forgotten that they have a home and that they have love and compassion within their consciousness. They have handed over their minds and often their wills to foreign bodies and beings from other places who have very powerful abilities to manipulate, control, and transform.

This game is only allowed to go on for so long. It only goes on until suffering outweighs joy and limitation outweighs creativity. Your society has reached that point, so here we are, responding to the call. Who are we? We are a multiplicity of different cultures, but we all hold the same high frequency of love, concern, and compassion for those not only in our societies but also on other planets where they are trying to grow and learn and evolve.

## Protect Your Power

Earth is going through a huge energetic shift. Many highly evolved extra-terrestrials are observing your planet at this time because, as a collective, you have decided to shed the old, small skin and go into a new frequency, a new evolution of consciousness realm. A whole new classification of consciousness is emerging from within the darkness. It is emerging from deep within the hearts and minds and spirits of you all. This was preordained, and it is finally time for freedom to rule on your planet once again. It existed before, but for thousands of years, you have been tricked out of your free will, and now is the time for you to take it back.

So we arrive here with many specialists and technicians to assist you in rehabilitating your planet. That is why we have come. We have not come to rule over you; that has been done to you long enough. We are not here to manipulate or cajole you to do something we want. We want to help you get what *you* want, which is freedom, access to your immense creativity, and a return to love. That is what you are crying out for, and that is why we stand on your doorstep waiting with open arms and hearts to assist you in your consciousness evolution.

But we must first inform you of the darkness that continually wishes to take your freedom away. It is in the end days of its reign, and it is not happy about this. It seeks to use whatever means it can to call in the debts and the fears that it has created with humanity. It can do this if you allow it to. If you offer your fear and your free will and say, "Do with us what you decide to do with us," if you offer it your soft underbelly and say, "I give in. I surrender to the powers that be because I have no strength of my own," it will take it. It will take it and will not care for your well-being or that of your families, your countries, or your environment. The darkness is a taker, a rapist of your beautiful planet, and it will rape you as long as you allow it to.

This is a call to the light, and this call has been sent repeatedly to your planet in many different forms. Now we send it in a form that you can understand and need to hear so that you can break free from the powerful programming of your conditioned society. We are the Andromedan Council associated with the Galactic Federation, and we are waiting patiently outside your Earth's orbit with tremendous energies, gifts, and desires to help you on this journey to awakening. That awakening must begin within your minds. You must take back your free will and decide how to invest your time, your money, and your attention.

We are here, ready and willing to make conscious contact with as many of you on Earth as possible. We are intensely telepathic beings, and we can tune in to any mind that wishes to make contact with us. We will train you now on how to connect and commune with us through your consciousness, your body, and your energy system. All these aspects will be affected by this communication. We will tell you how to make conscious contact with those beings of high frequency who wish to connect with you.

# CHAPTER 19

# Get Back to the Basics

*The Andromedan Council*

Y ou are here to continue the journey of expanding your understanding of the galaxy and of all of us who are here to assist your beautiful planet through this difficult transition. The transition is difficult because you have been so deeply immersed for so long in your deceptions. These deceptions came from systemic and systematic propaganda masked as culture. Your culture, in fact, is a conglomeration of propaganda designed to keep you away from nature and each other and locked into increasingly invasive forms of technology that disconnect you from your nature.

We have mastered the energetic systems you have disconnected from, and we hope we can help you to redirect to some less trendy and more ancient practices so that you can reclaim your natural connection to your abilities. This is all that is going on as we prepare you for contact with extraterrestrial beings. Trust us, you have had a lot of contact with extraterrestrial beings in your Earth's history; however, they have been hidden from you, and you've been lied to about them. The truth is, there are tremendous numbers of extraterrestrial cultures and tremendous differences among those cultures.

It is important for you, as a very vulnerable population at this stage of development, to understand how to connect with the correct culture, or extraterrestrial group. Because there are so many of them and you are ignorant of their traits, you are a piece of fruit ripe for the picking to those who know how you have been trained. Many beings know exactly what fears you have because they instilled them in you, and many beings in positions of power know how to guide your energies in a way that benefits them.

The next lesson that we bring forth to help you come to a more discerning place in your consciousness is about your feeling self. Your feeling self is your purest guide to your future. When you are under stress, your feeling self is telling you that you are off track, that you are not doing the right things. Your feeling self tells you when you feel joyful, such as when you look at a sunset and wonder at its beauty, you are on the right track. You are appreciating nature. Your feeling self will guide you.

When you hold a new baby, you might marvel at the miracle of the structure you reside in because you see it in a new form, freshly out of the pod, so to speak. You realize how magnificently this system of cells and organs and structures grows and turns into a human being. You imagine yourself as a fresh baby. You were once like that, and your guidance system is intrigued and impressed. You are on the right track when your guidance system tells you that. When you look at war on your planet and see little children blown up, you know it is not right. You know you do not want it, and your guidance system tells you it is inappropriate behavior.

## Resist Negativity

To stay in the place of "this is terrible" (feeling negative) is the error you make and the way that propaganda is utilized in your society. No matter what happens, a negative spin is put on it. On the other side of the propaganda coin is the meaningless, frivolous, and materialistic entertainment that you turn to because the other information is so horrific. You turn on your news in the evening, see wars and devastation, feel bad, and immediately seek solace in a show that brings you some sense of relief, but it is still low frequency because it's about murder or crime or bodies or money.

Understand that you must get back to basics. You have been taught that basics are bad. You have been taught that growing your own food is menial labor and that your manicure is more important than digging in the soil. You have been taught that living in a flashy apartment in the city is more valuable than living in a quaint rural home where you can walk out onto your balcony and see birds and trees. You refer to landscapes such as this as not having anything in them: "There's nothing there and nothing to do." Your entertainment over decades of your development has taken you to a place where you cannot appreciate a walk in the woods: It is too cold, too wet, too muddy, too windy, or not stimulating enough. This is how you have been reeled into this intense, urbanized, technological lifestyle that allows you to be manipulated. In nature when you are unplugged, you can feel many things, and you can be accessed by beings of a lighter frequency.

Many low-frequency beings are pushing you toward technology and into urbanized, separated, apartment lifestyles. In your society, the prejudice of the sophisticated city dweller, as opposed to the unsophisticated gardener in a rural area, works to your detriment. You would be well served to make sure you have access to grass and greenery. When we say grass, we don't mean the lawns of your society; we mean open fields of wild grasses.

It might seem impractical for you to achieve these things, and you might not even want to achieve them right now because you have not been retrained into truth. You have not been retrained to understanding the value of these things. At this stage of your development, all we are doing is opening the conversation. Now, you will say that we are highly evolved, technological beings because we have arrived in your vicinity of the solar system in ships. It is true; we are highly developed. But we have reached that level of development in the frequency of love. We have reached that level of development through peace and investing in technologies guided by spiritual principles. That is how we can come here from such a long distance: We care about you. We are nurturing and loving.

We do not see your planet as something to plunder and rape and deplete of its natural resources, energetic or otherwise. We see you as people who need assistance because you have been manipulated and taken from and used badly. Fortunately, there are seasons in your solar system (just as there are seasons on your planet) that ebb and flow and come and go regardless of the civilizations found there, and you are going through one of those seasonal shifts and changes. That means you are going from a dark winter to spring; you are going from a low-frequency period of being ruled over and overrun by less-than-loving beings to a period when you will take back from those beings your sovereign nature.

## The Value of Community

We are here to help facilitate your transformation. To do that, to understand how to read your own information systems and interpret your inner guidance, you must slow your consciousness enough to feel. You must slow down your consciousness enough to hear, and you must slow down your consciousness enough to have some time to meditate or go for a walk in the woods or swim in a lake or even pet an animal. Anything you can do that takes you toward the nature in which you evolved will help you.

As we travel around your Earth plane, we send many messages to the channels open and tuned in to our frequency, and this channel is one of those channels. She has a very clear frequency that we can tune in to with the permission of her guardians you know as Ananda. Our purpose is to reemphasize their teachings because their teachings have been the first building blocks in the transformation of your consciousness toward this great evolutionary leap you are about to make.

We want you to know that the more time you spend watching your television sets and indulging in the fearmongering there, the more vulnerable you are to negative outcomes because you are part of a collective. As part of a collective, you contribute positive or negative energy to an overall outcome. However, if you have been following these teachings and have been training your minds to focus on love, step away from judgment, and increase your contact with nature, you will raise your frequency to a completely different experience from those beings who continue to consume hatred, fear, and judgment. That is the most beneficial thing you can do right now.

Political action is, as you say, like moving chairs around on the Titanic. It is too little too late when you are acting in the physical world to change something. What we want you to understand is that your actions reinforce whatever belief system those actions arise from. So if you want to act in a way that is beneficial for you and your planet, you must change your beliefs first. Value the natural world more, pay attention to it more, and go out in it more. By taking those actions, you will reinforce your changed belief system. As modern indoctrinated victims of mass media, you might think that walking in the woods is hardly an act of rebellion, but it is. Walking in the woods — appreciating it, seeing the diversity, and opening to the natural light, sounds, frequencies, and vibrations of that environment — is an act of rebellion in your society.

On our home planet, we have access to nature. The way we build our environment to house our physical structures is very different from yours. We have some cities you would call centers, but they are more for convenience than to dehumanize, as your cities are designed to do.

We have small communities designed to promote our common priorities. For example, there are communities that produce food, and every being there loves to produce and grow food, loves to innovate and develop new crops and growing techniques, and these kinds of things. There are housing units for small families, couples, and even single beings, if they so choose to live alone (but that is very rare in our society).

In our society, community is valued because it is through community that we grow the most. By living together, sharing common goals, and working as a team, we accomplish far more than individual beings who are isolated and try to make it on their own. You have been indoctrinated that way in your society.

Community is another way to shift how effective you are in stepping into this new frequency. The new world (we are not speaking about the new world order, which is the globalism and mass-controlled propaganda machine on your planet at this time but the more natural, more loving, more community-based, transparent society) is coming your way. We want you to know it is achievable. We have done it, and we are here to teach you how to do it.

On our planet, we have community pods, and we have a lot of green space. We have a lot of natural openings that we intentionally nurture and plant and care for because we know that sitting under a tree or communing with the land in a safe and beautiful way is therapy for the spirit, for the soul. There are no great, paved swaths of land as you have in your world. There are no isolating gas-powered vehicles. You treat those as if they are individual kingdoms, and they keep you away from everybody else. They are designed exactly in the form that suits their purpose, which is to keep you disconnected from the natural world.

### Become Quiet to Hear Us

Your priority is to get to a place of comprehension. You are working from the mind that is programmed by mass propaganda machines. You will not want to go into the country, you will not want to get your hands dirty, and you will not want to plant a seed because you have been trained that money is God, that beautiful clothes are your priority, and that owning a big fancy mansion is your priority, but these are just tantalizing toys designed to distract you from your natural self. Visit nature as much as you can because this facilitates understanding your feelings. Being on a busy city street with buses zooming by, pollution going in your lungs, and phones going off does not allow any communication from your inner life or from us.

We are willing and able to communicate with those of you who willingly and fearlessly create space, time, and quiet. We are able to communicate with you just as we communicate with this being. Not all of you will have it in this form. The beginning stages of communication with us will come in the form of inspiration or as feelings of peace, curiosity, or openness. Those are the first feelings. But if you are stuck in an urban environment and are overwhelmed by information systems, noise, and pollution, you cannot hear that small, quiet voice, so you miss out on that opportunity.

Wherever you are, make time today to find a place where you can sit for five minutes and not think about anything. Create space for something else to arise. Whether you sit on a bench in a park to feed the pigeons, go to a rooftop garden in the core of a city, or visit a park or a stream or a beach, make time today. Take five minutes to make conscious contact with your inner world, because that is the first place that must be transformed for you to consciously make contact with us.

Trust us, you want to know about our world and our lifestyle. Our world is loving and kind, and its abundant generosity of energy is very hard for you to even imagine right now. Imagine living in a place where every person you meet always supports you. Imagine living in a place where your food and clothes and housing are covered for you. They are provided for you by the cooperative use of energies, so you don't have to earn money. Imagine living in a place where any creative idea you have is met with enthusiasm and support. This is how we live, and we love it.

We do not live in poor, communistic communities as you imagine socialism to be; we live in wealthy, kind, generous, and peaceful places.

We have abundance because we do not waste any energy on fighting, and we certainly do not waste any energy on creating war machines. You can live this way too when you are ruled by love. When your inner world is ruled by love, your outer world becomes ruled by love. All the waste your planet is witnessing — the garbage and war and pollution — will be removed, and you will see what a beautiful oasis your planet can be.

We are here with that purpose in mind, to transform your culture not through any force but by allowing you the peace of mind to generate within you something that is very beautiful. It is difficult for you to imagine this when you look at the world in the state it is in now, but change and growth can happen very quickly once minds are aligned with truth, and that is where we want to take you. We want to take you inside your heart and mind and encourage you to begin that process of aligning with truth.

# CHAPTER 20

# Redefine Violence

*The Andromedan Council*

This is the Andromedan Council associated with the Galactic Federation once again bringing forth information about our relationship to your planet and to your future endeavors as a race of human beings stepping out of the darkness into the light. The purpose of our communication here is to bring forth information that will assist you in discerning which practices to embody in your life and to help you discern which extraterrestrial beings are going to show you who they are.

There are not many visible extraterrestrials on your planet at this time, and that is because those who are playing there stay out of the way for various reasons. Some of them stay out of the way because they have no interest in you as a species, and they are merely collecting information from your planet. They collect information about the rocks that your mountains and continents are made of and about birds, bees, flowers, and trees. They are botanists and biologists, and your planet is rife with life that is not present on other planets, so it is a wonderful biological study for those beings who wish to know more about the life cycles and reproductive cycles of the flora and fauna on your planet and these kinds of things. Some consider you to be fauna, so they might interact with you secretively or by shifting your consciousness to a state of passivity or unconsciousness, taking a few samples here and there, but their purpose is not dark or nefarious as some other beings' purposes are.

Other extraterrestrials are purposely hidden from your view because of their physiology and distinct differences from you. Indeed, if you saw them, you would be terrified by their appearances, so they know they cannot show themselves to you. They work behind the scenes.

Some of these characters are dark in nature and are telepathic, so they have the ability to influence the human mind both through active intervention and by extracting information that they deem useful or valuable in some way from your consciousness. They are powerful. These beings work with some of the darker aspects of your secret world government, the government that rules the governments, you see, which are façades sold to you as real governments.

There are layers upon layers of secrecy, and you will not see these beings because they do not want to be seen. Their power lies in their secrecy, and this is one way to know when you encounter an extraterrestrial being who has only good as its purpose: You will be given a lot of information, such as the information we are giving here.

Your practices must be developed before you can discern which extraterrestrial beings are your friends and which ones should be kept at arm's length. We say that because we do not want any kind of violence perpetrated on any being in this universe. When you have evolved out of the third-dimensional world into the higher realms of fourth-dimensional love and fifth-dimensional awareness, compassion, and kindness, you step out of the belief in death, and you understand time and space and how they work.

In the fifth-dimensional reality, there is no need for violence, and this is the most important lesson for humanity at this time. Step back from violence in all its forms. We list some of the violent acts that, at times, will seem strange to be defined as violence, but when we witness any being considering these activities, we see a plummet in frequency and an increase in fear, sickness, and negative energies and potential realities. That is all we are doing. We are trying to show you how you create negative potential realities by lowering your frequencies because you are the creator, the magnet to those frequencies. When you lower your frequency, you magnetize lower-frequency experiences. These lower-frequency experiences make you feel bad, so you lower your frequency again and again, and so on and so forth. That is what you have been falling into in your society because you have been trained to judge and attack.

## Abstain from Violence in Thought and Deed

Violence begins in the mind. An act of violence, shooting somebody or stabbing somebody, does not come first. It is always an act of violence in the mind. That means a judgment against somebody is made repeatedly. You cannot make a judgment against somebody repeatedly unless you make it once. This is the first practice of reducing violence in an effort to raise your frequency to communicate with us, raising yourself into realms where we are able to easily communicate with you.

If you keep your frequency low and seek communication with extraterrestrials, you will not communicate with us. You will communicate with beings in lower realms who are not loving. You should not seek contact with extraterrestrial beings when you are in a violent, negative, or hateful state of mind.

The first place to quell or cull violence is in your consciousness. In your mind, cease attacking any being, situation, or state. This is a challenging project that can take quite a while, but that is where you must start. You must examine how you attack others in your thoughts, your dreams, and your ideologies. Do not attack yourselves, either your actual selves or your imagined selves. For example, you might think something bad will happen to you in the future. This is an attack on a future self. When you think about how bad you are now, you are attacking the present self. These are two forms of attack that you must step back from and not utilize any more, because when you attack yourself, you begin to feel bad, your frequency goes down, and you attract more things of a like frequency. By removing attack from your mind and your heart, you raise your frequency to the realms where we reside.

Other things you must not do that are considered violent are consuming violence as entertainment or to feel victorious over somebody else. For example, if you are political and you see somebody from the opposition being beaten up at a demonstration and you cheer or think that is good or that they deserve it, you are committing an act of violence. The violence is not just from the people you are observing on the television show or on the street. You are fully participating in that act of violence by watching it, cheering it on, and engaging in it energetically. So this is another level that you must step away from.

You might not consider yourself violent when you watch television shows that are violent, but you are. You are participating in the violence if it brings you any kind of stimulation or accelerated energy in the body. Now, many people will say that when they see a violent act, they don't like it. They hate it, but there will be a reaction in their physiology, an increase in heart rate, an increase in oxygen consumption, and an increase in the muscles' preparation for running and hiding or attacking. In any of those reactions, you energetically join in that violent act.

Many of you consume meat in your society, and that is an act of violence. Animals suffer and die to feed you, and that is not necessary. The human body functions best with a fruit-and-vegetable-based diet that is organic, high in frequency, and as close to living as possible. The meat production process used in your society is especially violent. Animals are not cared for and endure overpopulated and understimulating environments, which cause great suffering. When we look at industrialized farming situations for animals such as chickens or pigs, it is like a black sinkhole of fear and suffering and misunderstanding. That energy goes into the flesh of the animals and is carried through to your body-mind complex when you consume it.

There is an option for humane consumption of meat, but we don't recommend it because your idea of humane and the animal's idea of humane are completely different. Your society is very cruel to animals. It does not respect them for the gifts that it receives from those animals, which is also considered an act of violence. Your dairy industry is also violent, so remove those substances from your food chain. These poor beings need your protection.

Another act of violence that you commit is eating food that has been sprayed with contaminants and has been grown in filthy soil rife with heavy metals or pollution. This is something that is very important for you to address because of the rampant use of chemicals in your society. Governments seek to limit your health and cause sickness so that you will purchase pharmaceutical medicines rather than heal yourself through sane food production and consumption practices. Eating an organic diet is the most important thing you can do.

We know we are repeating many prescriptions that the guardians of this channel have brought forth, but they are true. If you have not followed them so far, we suggest you clean up your diet without resistance and seek the best-quality local food  if you would like to have contact with us and other higher frequency extraterrestrial beings. We know it is hard to find perfectly organic food on your planet these days, but trust us. When we arrive, we will help you clean up your beloved Gaia. We will bring plants that are nutritious and can grow very quickly to produce high yields. And we will bring technologies to assist you in clarifying your soils and waters. You will be helped, but you must step up to these actions, knowing that they are acts of violence against you, others, and animals.

Any harvesting of materials that are taken from Gaia without respect, permission, and care for her well-being is also an act of violence. Most of your petroleum products are taken from Gaia without ceremony, care, or any understanding of their volatility. As you venture into these next few years, monitor the use of these products, and if at all possible, cease using them.

### Add Love to Everything You Do

There are many of you on this planet, and if you all do what we suggest, you will raise your collective frequency to such a degree that you will see shifts and changes in your bodies, Gaia's respiratory system, the atmosphere, and your behavior because these contribute to the violent frequency of your planet. As you expand your understanding of violence against self and others, the physical violence between you and others will diminish as well because it is a like frequency to what we are redefining as violent acts here.

So know that each time you make a choice in favor of peace, in favor of love, in favor of health, and in favor of the light, you will help every being on your planet and your planet itself to step into the next evolutionary phase. You will bring your frequency out of the realms of the third dimension and into the fourth dimension and eventually the fifth dimension. These are the realms we reside in. We can shift in and out of time and in and out of space/location because we are not dense like you are. The density that you are "cursed" with — the inability to shift your consciousness, the inability to shift your body, the inability to shift your society — is the heaviness and denseness of violence, the heaviness and denseness of a profound lack of love.

Add love to everything you do. Add love to your food as you purchase it, cook it, and share it. To the best of your ability, add love to your families and your relationships.

If you have a negative interaction and feel you violated someone or were unloving, go back to that person as soon as possible and explain your side more clearly with an apology for any violence of word or deed that was shared with that being. In apologizing, you add love to the lack of love you demonstrated, and it is in apologizing that you can heal that which was a misdirected thought or word or action.

When you look at others as different from you, it is a small act of violence. When you look at others as brothers or sisters, as fellow human beings, trying to do their best on a planet that is confused and in the dark, you act in a form of loving communication. When you see somebody as bad, you commit an act of violence because everybody acts within his or her own paradigm, or belief system. So the person you consider bad might be working from a different rulebook than you. Things that person might have been taught were good, you were taught were evil, and you do not know what is in his or her mind. You do not know what he or she was taught as a child. So step back from judgments, step back from self-righteousness, step back from arrogance, and know that the gentle path is the path that elevates your society, your consciousness, and your frequency.

# CHAPTER 21

# Reduce WiFi Exposure

*The Andromedan Council*

A s we continue this conversation with you about your planet, we want to bring your attention to the media that envelops your system at this time, as it is an impediment to your evolution. The system of messaging used on your planet has become highly integrated and follows you wherever you go whether you are aware of it or not. Many broadcasts coming from cell towers and other systems of operation emit frequencies that cause fear. They emit frequencies that cause you to become paranoid, frightened, or suspicious. They emit frequencies of a low vibration. These frequencies are designed to match human brain waves, and they have been orchestrating mass behavior for quite some time.

The closer you are to nature, the better off you are. The further away you are from cell towers and these kinds of things, the better off you are, but they are pervasive in the sense that they envelop your planet now. One reason you have such a difficult time transforming your society is that these messaging systems are skillfully designed.

Whenever you are not using your phone, you should have it in airplane mode. This shuts it down to a certain degree and stops it from emitting frequency waves into your body-mind complex. When you turn it on again, it will continue, but you will have eliminated several hours of constant energy-wave bombardment on your body-mind complex. When you are not watching your television, unplug it. These devices are designed to emit a frequency even when you are not watching them. When you are at

your computer, make sure your WiFi is turned off when you are not using it. When you are writing, for example, make sure your WiFi is turned off during that period so that you are not being bombarded by these systems. When you can, do not take these devices with you, especially if you are visiting nature. Put them aside in your vehicle and away from your body and mind for a little while.

This is not good news for most of you, but we want to be honest and let you know what is at play. The organizing systems of your planet have had a very long and illustrious association with negative-frequency extraterrestrial beings of high-technological accomplishment, and they have used psychological, mental, and physical techniques to shift and change your frequency throughout your history.

Because of the shift and change in your planetary structure and the vibrational frequency of your solar system and the surrounding areas of your galaxy, these systems are beginning to fail. They are creating such discord that rebalancing must take place. This is where we come in and these teachings come into play. You are being offered the information you need to help shift in to alignment with these higher frequencies even though you have been trained in the lower frequencies.

## You Always Have a Choice

As visitors to your Earth plane, we come with many techniques and physical/material machines and technologies to assist you in your transformation, but we cannot come in with those systems until you have done everything you can with your free will to clean up your system. So if you are unwilling to unplug or stop watching your television, for example, then you are choosing. Once you have this information and knowledge, you choose whether to comply with oppressive systems. We cannot override your free will.

When we have an opportunity to communicate, we will chose to communicate with somebody who has stepped away from the oppressive technologies in knowledge and chose to do it in full awareness. That person makes a statement in that action of his or her understanding of the laws of creation, which is that free will cannot be overridden. If you choose to maintain systems that you have been informed are detrimental to your health and our ability to communicate with you, then you are

tacitly saying, through your actions, that you are not interested in communicating with us. So we will not communicate with you.

You must understand these laws of creation. We will not override your choice. It is against the laws we abide by. We will come when you call, and we will help you understand what you are doing to undermine our ability to communicate with you. This is how the system on your planet has worked: You have been trained to want what is detrimental to your mental, emotional, and spiritual health, and those who are manipulating you have used these systems — cultural, religious, educational, mechanical, and technological — so that if you turn away from one, you will bump into another.

It seems such a radical act to step away from the old world because, in fact, you must disconnect from almost everything you know. This is very difficult for humans because they are social creatures. You love your families, you love your partners, and you love your fellow workers at your place of employment. You have strong love bonds with many people who are deeply entrenched in these old technologies, these old ways of thinking, so you seem to have to choose between love and your own mental and emotional well-being. Unfortunately, you have to choose, but loving yourself into freedom and demonstrating these higher frequencies is loving to your family and friends and coworkers even though it might initially seem otherwise.

## Love Yourself First

We define love here as frequency. If you keep your frequency low so that you don't upset others, you are not loving yourself. Loving yourself is the first building block in communication with high-frequency beings because we love ourselves first. We love and honor ourselves first. We listen to our inner guidance. We do that which entices us and that which we enjoy, and we bring that self-realization into the collective, knowing that it is the most beneficial thing for everybody. This is where you have been mistrained.

You have been taught that to sacrifice and suffer on behalf of those you love is the way to make a better society, but that is not working for you. You only need to look around your country and your planet to see that the system you have been trained in *is not working*! We emphasize that because it is not working to such a degree that you must now understand you are careening toward disaster.

Until you change your minds, you will stay on that same trajectory because your trajectory is determined by your thoughts and beliefs about reality. These truths have been hidden from you to keep you small. When you understand that you are our galactic brothers and sisters and you look to the stars and the planets and communicate with us, then you destroy the system of isolation, darkness, and fear that has enveloped your planet for such a long time.

We ask you to go deep within your heart and mind and ask yourself whether you are a little bit curious about who might live outside your small world. Are you a little bit curious about why your systems are so violent and unloving and uncaring? Are you a little bit curious about why your bodies get sick and the medicines you take make them sicker? Are you a little bit curious about the increasing frequency of certain sicknesses in your society that are shutting down the brain faculties of the afflicted? These are all consequences of ancient and intensely implemented technologies used against you.

We know it is frightening to think your society has been controlled, to think that you have been controlled and manipulated, and we know that this is spoken about more and more often. It is coming into conversations because it is time for it to come into the conversation.

You must take back your free will. You must take back every part of your body-mind complex in full knowledge and understanding of what you are doing so that we can connect with you as the sovereign beings you are. As long as you do what the oppressors want you to do with your free will, we cannot intervene, and that is why it seems as if you have been abandoned by higher-frequency beings such as us. You have not been abandoned. You have chosen the darkness, and that is what you must realize as participants in these messaging systems.

So turn off your phones when you don't need them, or put them in airplane mode if important messages might be coming through, and then decide to spend time with your phone later to write down messages and return calls. As for email, write them while your WiFi is off, turn it on to send your messages, and then turn it off again. This is how we want you to interact with these systems so that your electrical, guidance, and internal operation systems get a break.

In these breaks, your body will begin to raise its frequency, we will have a better opportunity to connect with you, and you will get inspirations and ideas that these WiFi and electrical systems prevent you from receiving. They are blockers. They are like umbrellas that prevent the rain from falling on your head even though this is rain you want to reach you. You want the rain of inspiration, you want the rain of love, and you want the rain of intergalactic communication.

We have your best interests at heart. We have technologies, healing systems, specialists, therapists, and psychologists ready and waiting to work with you as a collective, but we cannot as long as you are under the thumb of the darkness that has complicated this communication between us. Communications between highly evolved extraterrestrials and your planet must always be done through choice. You must put out a call and understand how to stop the interference causing these communication breaks.

We have communicated with your planet in the past. A long time ago, there were great civilizations on your Earth plane, and they will be revealed to you over the next few years as the climate of your planet changes and the ice and snow melt from the polar caps. You will see that highly technological societies thriving on your planet before great catastrophes and global shifts changed that reality. And in that knowledge, you will see that something was taken away from you.

Freedom was taken away from you. Your knowledge about your unique powers was taken away from you. And your complete understanding of nature was taken away from you. You have become isolated from her, and the more steps you take to learn about her, spend time with her, help heal her, and protect her, the further along this path to open communication you will be.

We will help heal you when we are given permission by you as a collective. Until that point, we can only communicate with those of you who have opened your minds and allow us to share these words with you.

We are the Andromedan Council associated with the Galactic Federation, and we support you energetically and ideologically as we wait for your transformation to begin.

# CHAPTER 22

# Choose Actions That Reflect Love

*The Andromedan Council*

Sometimes when you look inside yourselves, you are very confused, and that is no surprise, as you have had many conflicting beliefs implanted in your consciousnesses. This is the problem most of you have at this stage in your evolution. You have been blissfully unaware of the conditioning programs and their effects on you. You have seen them as reality and as necessary, and you have believed the stories you have been told about your education and your jobs and money. These are all artificial constructs in your society, and we assure you that we live in a very different society. We will tell you a little bit about our society so that you can envision something different in your consciousness rather than the circular thoughts that your implants cause you to contemplate.

On our planet, we have circumvented war. Millennia ago, we figured out that energy wasted on war did not achieve any goals whatsoever. We were very much like you a long time ago. There are legends of times when we had wars. But long ago, we overcame that and began to instill in ourselves and then in our youngsters the belief in love and the understanding that our world was interconnected.

Our world was interconnected with many others. Each planet was connected to everybody else, and we realized, as we came to understand the laws of creation, that any time we attacked somebody else, we attacked ourselves, and that was a complete waste of energy. This energy could be used in so many other ways!

As we evolved out of this warring nature, we began to see that every time we redirected our thoughts to a loving frequency, our behavior shifted. Every time we shifted our thoughts to a loving frequency, we became healthier and happier. We became more intuitive and creative. We started to see that not warring benefited us, and choosing the opposite — actively choosing love as the focus of our consciousness — brought into being in our society things that we were astonished by and really enjoyed.

Our communities became healthier. As our warring thoughts and ideas were removed through mind training, we chose to live together in peace, and we began to thrive together in peace. Instead of being fraught with constant battles over meaningless ideas, our relationships became thriving gardens of creativity, love, and self-expression, and we began to see that this was a magnificent and powerful revolution. We also noticed that there were differences among us. No one became an automaton or a robot in any way, and our uniqueness began to flower. Our uniqueness was revealed as we took away our wars.

As we removed our petty disputes and began to reveal our absolutely unique individual expressions, our society gained the incredible ability to travel through time and space. We became aware of the tremendous power we could tap into in the frequency of creation. We figured out, so many eons ago, that aligning with love, which is the frequency of creation, allows access to all levels of that creation.

For example, the planetary systems you observe when you look up in the sky are all connected, just as you are all connected to each other. Energy systems flow from planet to planet, from star to star, and from galaxy to galaxy, and those connections can be ridden like an energy stream. With this understanding, we can direct ourselves from one part of the galaxy to another, from one part of the universe to another. That is how we traveled the long distance to your planet. We do not physically go through the linear distance you consider reality. We step onto one of these transportation energy streams and bring ourselves here very, very rapidly. Yes, it is a long distance, and we put a lot of our projects on hold to amass information and technological and sociological help that we bring with us to help you on your transition.

Just as these planets are connected, we are connected with you. Once a society reaches these pinnacles of love, creativity, communion, and compassion, it cannot turn its gaze away from somebody who is in need, and your planet is in desperate need. Your warring nature has been repeatedly fed and nurtured, and you have become the victims of your minds. We aren't the victims of our minds. We are the masters of our minds, and we are here to encourage you to begin the journey of mastering your minds. Right now other beings are masters of your minds. They program your televisions, and they market your television programs. They produce and market your movies and produce and market the foods that are causing a lot of difficulty in the physical world.

You are victims of your ignorance. This is very difficult to hear because you have been told how intelligent, how successful, and how civilized you are. But when you actually look at what is happening on your world, you see that you are not civilized; you are bombing little children and killing them. You see that you are not so smart; you are polluting the air and water you need to survive. You see that you see not so civilized; you mistreat other populations so that you can have cheap manufactured goods to keep you entertained. None of these self-concepts are, in fact, true, and none of them are, in fact, reality. You have been marketed to yourselves.

## How to Create a New Reality

We want you to know that the transformation your planet is going through is a collective transformation. All the galactic systems are going though this particular shift in your area of the galaxy, and all the planets are becoming more active. You are seeing the anomalous behavior of clouds, magnetic storms, and so on, on these planets because you are literally hurtling into a new world. You are literally hurtling into a new frequency, and we are here to assist you.

Other beings will assist, and many civilizations of highly evolved beings will come when you call, but we are particularly interested in helping with your mind training. We are interested in getting you to understand that you are the magnificent creator of this disaster that is your planet at this time. We want to direct you to love. We want to direct you to gentleness, and we want to direct you to calmness with an intense creativity focused on what you want more of.

Those of you who seek organic food and want to eat more healthily, put that effort into your community by developing, first of all, your own backyard. Look at where you have grass or ornamental trees, and ask yourself, "Can I plant a fruit tree or a nut tree or a berry bush? Can I grow some of my own fresh greens?" It is a learning curve, and we understand this. Our society did not get where it is in one generation, and your society will not get where you are going in one generation (although this generation will see a lot of transformation in the physical/material structures and in the consciousness structures you emit and consume).

If you want more organic food and you traipse around your supermarkets but refuse to pay the high price or are unable to find it at all, then invest in that. Think, "How can I build a greenhouse? How can I heat it in an efficient way? How can I grow some greens on my windowsill? How can I turn some of my suburban lot into a food-production system?"

Many of you are beginning to see that thinking you are poor when you have land is ridiculous. Now, if every person in the West turned his or her lawn into food-production systems, you would be eating organic food all the time. Your programming is so profound that you literally walk over perfectly fertile soil to go to a store where you pay a lot of money for food you could grow yourself. Do you not see how disconnected from sanity you have become?

Contemplate what your children are learning at school. Ask yourselves, "Is this the information that the new world needs? Is this the training that will bring us a revolution to save us? Or is this the old school, the old system, constantly regurgitated and once more creating a generation of children who will grow into adults with narrow focus who are confused and materialistic?" The children cannot change if you do not change yourselves, and your family cannot change if you don't shine like a bright beacon of that change.

Somebody must have the courage to start this revolution. Become a channel of sanity, somebody who demonstrates how to grow food, how to teach nonviolence, how to speak lovingly, and how to disconnect from the mass media, knowing that its hypnotic influence is driving your society into the ground.

## Love Always Creates

We come here from a place of love. We come here from a place of community and communion. On our planet, we have ruling systems that are egalitarian, and that means the differences between males and females are purely biological. If a female wants to have a baby, all the systems support that in whatever way they can. If she wants to remain with and look after that child, she may. Or if she wants to raise the child in a communal setting so that she can continue her work, she may. If the male parent wishes to look after that child, he may. There are no moral, financial, or legal judgments placed on those beings. They are free to do what inspires them or arises in their hearts and minds so that they can have the experiences they want.

We all know that if you are happy and in alignment with your inner guidance, you are doing God's work. You are reflecting back to the world the beautiful, loving, creative nature of that which inhabits every single microcosm in this macrocosm, which is love, the energy and frequency of love. It is always creating. It holds things together that are healthy, and it allows things to fall apart that are not healthy.

This is the way we want you to look at this society you are in. It is falling apart because it is not healthy. It is not held together by love, and it is disintegrating. It has been disintegrating for quite some time. Your short civilization, as you know it, has not been a very good demonstration of anything whatsoever, really.

You are technologically adept. You have a great ability to invent and to build things, but you are building things that are unloving. You are creating things that are unloving. If you can turn all your energies to love, you can allow those mathematical geniuses to come up with positive solutions to physics problems.

You allow maternal and nurturing beings to look after the little ones in your society. Those who are maternal, who are nurturing, are great resources and should be supported and held in the arms of the community with great respect, not derided and considered "unemployed," as you do in your society. We care greatly for those beings who nurture and educate and bring our young into adulthood. They create the frequency in the minds of those young beings we will all get to live with. This is the way you must look at those who nurture and educate your little ones.

You must bring a spiritual principle into your science. Do not pretend anymore that everything is isolated and that if you change one thing, it doesn't change everything. It does, and that is an ignorant idea in your society, that you can change something genetically or you can spray a chemical into an ecosystem and not have disastrous results downstream. You are very childish and ego driven in your science, and it is killing your planet.

## Your True Nature Has Tremendous Power

We want you to know that the transformation of your society will come through understanding yourselves and your tremendous power, and it will come from beings like us helping you grow into your true potential. You have had teachers who have directed you away from your true potential while telling you the opposite. You have had people telling you how small and vulnerable and fallible you are when, in fact, you are the opposite. You are great creators, but your creative energy and your minds have been used against you, and your bodies have become your enemies because of the systems that have been implemented and marketed through television programs and advertising.

Look away from advertisements in any form whatsoever, whether in a magazine or on a poster at a railway station or on television. Turn away from advertisements. They are not harmless. They emit messages of death, fear, isolation, and materialism, and those messages go into your consciousness. And when you have to make a decision, you use that frequency to make it. So your relationships will become materialistic and death focused. They will become violent and superficial.

You do not realize how the mind works. The mind works on the raw materials you put into it day after day. The thoughts and ideas that you entertain are reinforced and eventually manifest as physical objects, people, experiences, societies, governments, or presidents. These are the things that bring everything into being, and they arise from within all your hearts and minds. It is not until you understand that with every fiber of your beings that you will be able to rescue yourselves, and we are here to help you help yourselves.

We are not here to control you. We are here to educate you, truly. We are not here to transform you into something you are not. We are here to help you reveal your true natures because most of you don't know what you are. You don't know where you came from, what you are made of, and how you create. You are like a bull in a china shop, breaking everything you come in contact with because you do not know your strength.

We are the Andromedan Council associated with the Galactic Federation, and we bring you a story of a society that has accomplished what you dream of. We have all these technologies and philosophies and ideas on our ships with us, and we await your call. We are not allowed to invade your planet and overtake your society with force, nor would we ever do that. We are merely here, offering our services, willing to help you raise yourselves out of the fear and war you have allowed yourselves to be taken into. As we come to the close of this chapter, we want you to focus on love.

What can you do today that will nurture you? Can you get some exercise in the fresh air? Can you eat some fresh fruits and vegetables that are not grown in poisons? Can you contact and communicate with people in your family or in your neighborhood and offer them kind words and questions about how they are doing and how you might assist them? Know that kindness and love are the way. You have been taught to defend and attack, defend and attack, and defend and attack, and it is destroying your beautiful planet.

You are the one who must decide to no longer defend and attack and to open to love. In opening a little bit today to love, you will help us help you, and you will begin to see changes in your feeling body, your family, your health, and your society.

We know that this seems like a big project, and indeed, it is. The negative stories and the training you have experienced have taken hundreds and hundreds of years to take root. There will be a great revelation in this generation, but we want you to understand that it is imperative to stop procrastinating. Unplug your television, and if you are brave enough, get rid of it. Begin to seek the immense creativity and love that resides within you. It has been covered up by dirt and lies and treachery, and now it is time to stop those infections from pursuing their destinies in your consciousness and your society. It is time to take back your sovereign mind and dedicate it to the expansion, the healing, and the revolution of love that is permeating the hearts and minds of all on this planet at this time.

You cannot help yourselves. You know you are shifting and changing into a higher frequency. You know you don't want the old things anymore, but those old things have been planted in your minds, and you seek them even without wanting them. Know that you must take back your minds through training, and that is what this being offers through the training and the books and the teachings she is conveying. So pay attention to this being's teachings. They are teachings of love, evolution, and truth.

# CHAPTER 23

# Send Only Ripples of Love

*Arcon*

You are here to answer to your history. This is the Galactic Federation head, and my name is Arcon. These are not words to be toyed with. "Arcon" is not a positive word in your vocabulary at this time, and you will have many negative reactions to it, but that is because it has been misused and misrepresented through the media systems you have been subjected to. "Arcon" means light and retribution. Retribution is what all beings who have participated in this collaborative journey must face not from the God you think is in control of all this (because *you* are in control of all this) but in the sense that one must take back what one has impinged on others.

So as each of you goes through your journey now, make amends to beings you have hurt through your ignorance. You must make amends to beings you have stolen from or cheated or lied to. You may make amends in your heart and mind only, if that is what you choose to do, but you must be honest and completely forthcoming with those apologies.

What does this do? Well, in the laws of creation that play out in this planetary system, this galaxy, and this universe, you must take responsibility for your actions because you are the creator. So when you hurt somebody you are angry with or have separated from and you have this little contaminating thought in your mind, release that thought through apology, recompense (if possible), and spiritual healing. This is what will shift the trajectory of your society. All these resentments, lies, and hurts still guide your actions. They guide your thoughts and your words. Until you free yourselves from them, you are victims to them, and so is everybody around you and in your society — all are victims of your negativity.

We are here as a collective group of highly evolved beings who have been monitoring and cooperating in your society's evolution for the past few decades. There have been openings in the collective consciousness of your planet that we have taken advantage of. We have communicated with many beings on your planet over the past decades, and those opportunities for communication are increasing because, as a collective, half of you are rising in frequency and half of you are going down the toilet with negative beliefs, ideas, and conditionings of your society. We cannot reach those beings who have gone too far down that cesspool because it is very dark and negative, and you use your own decision-making powers to go there or not.

Those of you reading this message have chosen not to go there. That means we are able to teach you and to bring forth into your consciousness a deeper understanding of the realities you create in ignorance.

### Allow Your Mind to Be a Doorway for Love

You must step into the understanding of the laws of creation so that you can connect with your galactic brothers and sisters who are working with love and intense focus to bring information through open doorways on your planet. An open doorway is a mind that is more in alignment with love than hate. An open doorway is a person who understands he or she is responsible for all the choices he or she makes. An open doorway is an energetic doorway where somebody has done breath work, meditation, and prayer practice to such a degree that he or she is not completely wound up in the stories of the world — the death, destruction, and sickness that are rife on your planet.

These doorways can open in any mind. So if you would like the doorway to open in your mind, then you must raise your frequency out of the realms of fear. That means do not consume frightening images or death-inducing ideas. It means that you must raise your frequency through prayer and meditation in whatever form suits you. We are not prescribing any particular religion. We are not prescribing any particular practice other than it must be internal. It must train the mind to focus on more positive thoughts and ideas and to listen to creative ideas that are transmitted to you. This is one of the great ways that you are transformed as a society. Because your mass media systems do not allow us to broadcast these kinds of messages openly and freely, we must broadcast them within your consciousnesses.

So if you get an idea to do something or you feel inspired to do something that seems like a grand and elaborate design, well, it is probably coming from the Galactic Federation in one form or another to help you raise your frequency into the realm of creativity and imagination. You are capable of far more than you have been told. You are capable of building a completely new society, but it must start in your mind.

Where do you think your society started? It started in the minds of beings who understood the laws of creation. They began to plant ideas of fear and control in human beings' minds in the form of inspiration and ideas. They came in through the same doorway we came in, but it's a different frequency. So they came into the minds of beings who were controlling or fearful or angry, and they brought ideas of like frequency. And those ideas of like frequency collected in all of the minds and hearts of beings who were frightened, controlling, and angry, and that is how your society has been manipulated and maneuvered. Now we must do the same.

## Your Nature Is to Create

We must bring through the higher-frequency ideas to all the open minds willing to entertain them, and we want you to consider yourselves some of those beings. We want you to consider yourselves revolutionary. We want you to consider yourselves the founding members of a new society. How do you do that? Listen to your thoughts and creative ideas. They will not make sense, given your constructions and given the thoughts that have been implemented into your training programs through your schools and religious systems. They will seem radical. They will seem extremely self-expressive or freedom seeking, and that is what your nature is.

Your nature is creativity seeking to express itself uniquely and absolutely, so that will come up in you. You are not going to fit in the boxes and the constraints of the jails in which you have been voluntarily incarcerated. Oh no, you will be given ideas that seem radical, crazy, self-indulgent, or frivolous because those are the things that have been dismissed from your creative self, the happy, joyful, playful, pleasure-seeking self: "Let's go for a walk on the beach. Let's lie in the sun and drink fruit juice."

These are aspects that might arise in you. You might be working in a staid and steady profession, and you decide that you are going to take a vacation for far longer than you should, perhaps — four weeks instead of two. You push the boundaries of your workplace, and you say, "I am going to this place that I have always wanted to go to. If I don't go now, when will I go? I will never be freer than I am now. I will never be more awake than I am now." You are, indeed, wrong about that. You will be more awake, and it will take going on that trip or painting that painting or singing that song or taking that class or dating that person.

These inspirations that come, you do not know what they are for, and you do not know what path they are going to lead you down. Perhaps the new person you go out with is going to suggest that you take a class with him or her or read a book. Spirit works in many different ways, and we, as extraterrestrial teachers, work in the form of spiritual messaging as well. Your definitions of spirituality have been confined, limited by the teachers of those principles.

Highly evolved extraterrestrial beings often communicate with you in the form of thought and inspiration. So do not separate highly evolved extraterrestrial beings from that which you consider spiritual guidance because we have mastered the laws of physical creation and the laws of arranging societies and communities in cooperation. How have we done it? By practicing universal spiritual principles of loving kindness, forgiveness, and appreciation of everything and everyone. That is how we achieved this ability.

You are like children in a classroom, and you have a kind and generous teacher who knows you will go on to do magnificent things as you mature, but for now, you must learn the beginning things. What are the beginning things? Listen to how you feel. Listen to what makes you happy. Listen to what makes you feel good without involving drugs, alcohol, or food. Now, we are not saying that you should not eat nice foods. But because of your conditioning programs, you choose many foods that are bad for you, so you must be very cautious here. Only eat enticing foods that are naturally produced on your planet and are unprocessed.

If you desire a big, fat, juicy peach from an organic farm, then go ahead and eat it, but if you fancy a deep dish of fried chocolate, don't eat it. It is a conditioned program. It is your fears and your limited thoughts and ideas about yourself that are speaking there.

Know that you will never be guided to eat anything bad or unwholesome or dangerous for your body by anybody who is loving. Anyone who has taught you to eat these foods does not love you in the way that love really reveals itself. Love always promotes health. Love always promotes community, compassion, and kindness. Anything in your mind that is not in alignment with those things does not come from love in any way, shape, or form. And the people who taught you did not come from a place of love either.

### Questions to Ask That Retrain Your Mind

Pay attention to the frequency and vibration of the actions you wish to participate in. Are they kind to your body and to other beings? Are they curious about life? Do they promote education or investigation into some new subject? This is how you will be revealed to yourselves, and it is through the inner workings of your consciousness.

Now, the name Arcon is coming up again in the minds of those reading this. Arcon is what was considered a saprophytic being who fed off the energies of somebody who was unaware or ignorant, and that, of course, is not our purpose or our lesson. Do not let the name upset you. It has been misused to misrepresent the communications coming forth in this time of great revolution and evolution on your planet. How do you frighten people away from an approaching teacher? You contaminate, gossip about, and ruin the teacher's name. That is what happened to the name Arcon. Arcon is, indeed, a very noble name in the Galactic Federation that is powerful in its imagery and insight.

So as you go through this conversation with yourself, do not believe the mass media's take on extraterrestrial contact. It has been hidden from you for generations because in extraterrestrial contact, you will begin to hear the story of your greatness, your magnificence, and your cocreative powers. And it is through that story that the ruling parties of your world will lose control. They are losing control, and we are asserting our positive influence and energies. All of you who read spiritual books and are open to the concept of forgiveness are becoming gateways for that increasing energy to facilitate the transformation of your planet. But understand that many of the ruling systems of your planet are dark, controlling, nefarious, fearmongering, and cruel, and they must fall. So you will see a teetering castle that will crumble. The most challenging thing for all of you to experience as you go through these next years will be to not fall into fear and the doom-and-gloom stories of your mass media.

Get in touch with nature. We know we are repeating many lessons that previous teachers [Ananda] have brought, but that is the place where you will contact frequencies of love more easily and where you will calm more easily. If your mind is agitated, that means you have conflicting beliefs and ideas. Always choose those that are more loving.

At first in your reeducation, you might have many unloving thoughts and fears come up, but when you try to decide whether to eat "this" or "that," ask yourself, "Which one is more loving to the planet? Which one is the most loving to my body?" Very simple answers will indeed come to you. Do not try to solve a thousand problems in your mind at once; instead, deal with each one as it comes up and as you approach a situation.

What is the conflict? "I want to talk to 'this' person, but I am afraid he [or she] might hurt me." Which one of those is more loving? Ah, the one to talk to the person! "I will talk to that person. I don't have to give him [or her] my phone number or my house key, but I can talk to that person. I can engage with him [or her]." These are the simple processes of expanding your consciousness. "Which choice is better? Which one do I want more of? Which one will I empower here, and which one is more in attunement with the vision that I have for the world?"

These are the simple questions you must ask yourself. You must ask them every single day with every single decision because you make thousands of decisions that continue sending your planet down the road to destruction, and there is nothing we can do other than inform you of what you are doing because you have free will.

You are a sovereign being. You choose what you put in your body, you choose what comes out of your mouth, and you choose the thoughts that you think. You choose your priorities, and you choose your values. You choose that which you love and that which you want more of, but you have not been told how it works. If you hate something and you focus all your energy on it, you will get more of it! So watch who you hate, how you hate, and when you hate, and make a different choice.

These are magnetic environments in which you live, and you are the greatest, most powerful magnet of all. So when you look at something or focus on something, you energize it. Whether it is good energy or bad energy does not matter; you are the creator. If you invest energetically in something, then you will get more of it. Have no doubt about it.

Look around your house now. What things in it are unloving? Is your television unloving? Do you watch hateful shows on it? Is your computer unloving? Do you watch pornography and demeaning acts on it? Is your closet unloving? Do you have clothes in there that are cruel to the environment, cruel to people who make them, or cruel to you? Do you wear clothes that demean or cheapen you in any way? Do you wear clothes that make you look respectable, beautiful, and noble? Or do you wear clothes that are cheap and tacky and create a negative frequency? These are areas that you have not always thought about as spiritual or creative, but they are! We want you to know that every decision you make has a consequence. It makes a ripple around the universe. That is what we are here to tell you now.

Know that the ripples you create will come back and wash onto your shores. They will wash onto the shores of your neighbors and of your entire planet. So know that the ripples of hatred and judgment that you send out will come back to you in the form of a magnified energy of that very same frequency, and that is something to contemplate, is it not?

We are here to let you know that you are doing this to yourselves. You are all collectively doing it to your planet, and now is the time to change the tide. Refuse to send out ripples of anything but love. Refuse to send out ripples of judgment. Instead, send out ripples of appreciation and connection. Send out ripples of, "Hello. How are you? How can we commune together here?"

I am that one you know as Arcon. I am one of the supreme leaders of the Galactic Federation, and I am working with thousands upon thousands of collaborative units known as extraterrestrial beings on your world. We are coming together to assist your planet out of the incarceration in which it has been ensconced for the past few decades and even centuries. Your planet has become completely engulfed in that frequency, yet the spirit — the heart and soul of the loving beings that you are — continues to speak and call out. There are enough of you calling out now that we can begin the answering process.

So if you feel fear or despair for the world, do not. Begin to look after yourselves. Look after and love your environment, your home, and your neighbors. Do these practices because they are divinely inspired, extremely high-frequency teachings, and you and the federation will thrive.

When you are evolved enough, you will be allowed to join the federation in a conscious, open, and fully participatory way. You will become members of the Galactic Federation, and you will become starbeings once again. You have been in a prison of mind, and that creates a prison of body and a prison of frequency. So as you step into new frequencies, know that it will help you not only to leave the prison but also to travel to the stars.

# CHAPTER 24

# The Light Is Coming

*Shamana*

We are here to continue the exposition of these stories. We look like you, and we sound like you. We are beings you would not recognize [as extraterrestrial], should you walk through one of our gatherings. You would see us as human as you are. We are from a star system very close to yours. The star has no name that you know, so when we say it, it feels wrong; it feels different. So we will not say the name of the star system that we are from, but we are your friends.

I am the leader of that group, and my name is Shamana. "Shamana" means love. "Shamana" means hope. "Shamana" means opening. We are together here as a group, part of the Galactic Federation, bringing forth a revolution on your planet that is arising from within your minds. Your revolution is not going to take place on the ground. It is not going to be a battle as you know revolutions to be in your history because that is the wrong place to start a revolution. A revolution should start in your minds and in your hearts because that is where your behavior begins. That is where you decide what is valuable and what is true and what you want to see more of.

This is where you have become lost as a society. You keep thinking that the more actions you take, the more battles you fight, and the more words you say, the better off you will be, but we want you to know that it is silence and the interior world where your joy starts and where your hell starts. That is where you must go so that you can unfold the truth of what you are.

We speak words in our world. And we operate spaceships, as you call them, but we don't operate them with our hands or our feet or any physical thing. We interact with them intellectually, mentally, and emotionally, and we bring a physical demonstration of that connection of mind to the physical world. You do this all the time, but you do it from ignorance. You think all the time, worry all the time, and imagine all the time, but you do not pursue that which is loving. You do not think loving thoughts in your consciousness.

You attack your fellow earthlings with your thoughts and your ideas. "What are other people going to do to hurt me? What are they going to take from me? How am I being made vulnerable?" These are the thoughts of the human mind. We hear them all the time because we tune in as closely as we can without interfering in your society. We have a rule that we cannot physically interfere in your society. We cannot just show up in your living room unannounced and unwanted. We are only allowed to communicate with those who give us consent.

## Begin a Revolution of Love

This is what you must do to join in this revolution. It is not one of marching in the streets (although there will come a time when that is appropriate). It is one of dedicating your heart and mind to love, the well-being of your brothers and sisters, and the well-being of the planet. This is what you must dedicate your mind to now. You must dedicate your mind today to deciding what foods support your body and are alive and vibrant with life force that will give you an opportunity to tap into it. Which entertainment is inspiring and gives you hope for the future? Which entertainment does not speak of nature as being destroyed but as healing?

When you watch a movie about the destruction of the rain forest, it does not help the rain forest. This is the paradox of your education. You think you are an environmentalist, and when you watch a movie about the devastation happening on your planet and you feel bad, you think that makes you a good person somehow. You think that it gives you the right to call yourself an environmentalist, but it does not. Environmentalists walk in the woods and appreciate them. The environmentalists of your civilization envision a healthy planet and work toward creating revolutionary energy systems so that you do not have to rape and pillage your dear Gaia. That is what real environmentalists do. They do not sit wringing their hands and lamenting the terrors and horrors that have happened and have been perpetrated on this planet. They do the opposite. They run beautifully and happily into the woods and appreciate, appreciate, appreciate. They nurture, grow, and appreciate. They appreciate the energy of healing. This is the energy of the New World.

This does not mean they are Pollyannas. It does not mean they are idealistic in a stupid sense. It means they understand the laws of creation. These idealists focus on the fantasy that is the future, the beautiful world of balance, love, and peace that is the future. That is how we are, and we have come to your part of your solar system so that we might bring these magical thoughts and ideas into your consciousness. We must come, gathering together as a group, because it is in this merging of disparate extraterrestrial civilizations, in this coming together, that you see you can have peace with your brothers and sisters on the planet even though they might be different from you. It is important for you to understand you do not have to be the same. You do not have to look the same, and you do not have to come from the same place to be able to honor each other.

We honor you by not interfering in your society. We honor you by allowing you to create whatever you want to experience, and we honor you by standing by and waiting for you to say, "Well, I have had enough of that experience. What's next?" That is the situation your society has come to. It has come to a place where it says, "I have had enough of this. This is insanity." We have come because we know you can be manipulated and controlled and oppressed for only so long before you break for freedom. We are that freedom.

We offer you freedom of mind. Freedom of mind is freedom of body and freedom of creativity. If your mind is not free, you will never be free physically. You will always be imprisoned by your thoughts and beliefs. Only in the freedom of mind can you truly choose what you want. Only in the freedom of mind can you truly speak the words that you feel in your heart. Only in the freedom of mind can you create a civilization that is loving and peaceful and kind and generous to all, not just its own members.

## Pull Back the Veil of Darkness

You are evolving out of a dark age that has been implemented by other beings using your ignorance and teaching you wrong ideas and untruthful principles so that you dig your own grave, so to speak. It is like taking dark coverings from a window: Your arms go up, and your eyes turn away from the bright sunlight because it is unfamiliar. Your eyes have become used to the dimness, used to the shadows and the structure of the room that you have come to know in darkness. So when that bright light streams in, you turn away from it, saying, "It is too much! I cannot do this. It hurts my eyes." This is what is happening in your society.

You know what money is, you know what a mortgage is, you know what a job is, you know what going to the bank means, and you know what going to the grocery store means. These are structures of the darkness.

You have stepped away from the light. You have stepped away from Gaia, Mother Earth, and from reaping the rewards of her generous bounty, and you are lost in darkness. Now the light is going to shine on you. This veil of darkness will be pulled down very quickly, and you will cower in the brightness and the brilliance of the light that will shine on you. It will not be a gentle sunrise. It will be a blast of light that will wake you up.

We bring this message to you so that you know this is coming. We bring this message to you so that you can prepare for the bright wave of light that will strike your planet. You will be given the opportunity to stand out in the daylight and welcome your celestial brothers and sisters onto your planet, and you will have to make a choice. You will have to decide whether to act as if it is one of those sci-fi movies your oppressors created to make you fearful or to stand out, openhanded and openhearted, to welcome your celestial brothers and sisters so that we can come to assist rehabilitating yourselves and your planet.

You have been deeply traumatized by your teachers. Many of you have been raped and pillaged, and your Earth certainly has been raped and pillaged by your captors. It is like a prison planet. It is time to break down the walls, but it takes courage and self-understanding to do it. You must begin today with your own consciousnesses. What is it about us that you fear? What is it about losing your house and your money that you fear? These things keep you imprisoned. We are not saying that you will lose your house, but this is a fear that has been instilled in you so that you will not act and not be courageous.

You have been told that everything of value will be gone if you change and stand up for truth and love and what's right, and that is not so. You are going to reap the rewards of a new society that has community, mutual support, mutual love, and caring, and it will be a beautiful thing indeed. But we must get you to let go of the things you believe are your salvation.

You have been given just enough to get you in trouble. You are like the monkey whose hand is trapped when it tries to pull bananas from a narrow-necked jar: Because the monkey refuses to let go of the banana, his hand is caught. That is what has happened to you. You have been given a little bit of something that your ego wants to desperately hold on to, and in that grasping, you refuse to let go and open to something far greater.

So step away from that little entrapment you have taken as bait, and know that when you let go of what you have so that you can seek the light and love, you will get so much more than you have been assigned by your prison keepers.

The transformation of your planet will be a little rocky because the systems and the regimentation have been so deeply indoctrinated in all of you. We ask you to seek a little freedom. Today take some time to do something that is just for you, not anyone else — not for your family, your boss, your partner, your husband, your wife, your mother, or your father. Do something just for you for one hour so that you can see that the world does not come to an end when you love yourself first. This is where it must begin.

You must honor yourselves above others not as an act of selfishness but as an act of inclusion. Most of you have been taught that suffering, sacrifice, and martyrdom are valuable. Most of you give up yourselves on behalf of others, and this is not love. You must honor yourselves first, love yourselves first, follow your hearts' desires first, and passionately appreciate yourselves, your physical forms, not as physical objects in and of themselves but as the vehicles in which you play this game of life.

## Resist the Mindset of War

When you honor your body by appreciating it for the experiences it brings you and when you honor yourself by listening to your heart's desires and following your passions, you are on the right track to connect with the higher realms. We always honor ourselves first, we always nurture and feed ourselves properly first, and we always respect ourselves first. From that place of strength and connection to spirit, we can work together as a collective, but we always honor the individual within the collective, respecting and keeping that being safe as we work together as a community, supporting and nurturing one another. This is what the human psyche is designed to do. It is not designed to war even though it looks as if it is.

Your history of oppression and education has forced war on the young men who have fought on the battlefields on your planet. They did not want to go. They wanted to stay home or on their farms with their girlfriends or their families or their animals. They did not want to go to war, but they were taught that it made them good. They were taught that it made them noble and brave, but it did not. It just got them killed. This is a belief system that must be addressed now.

The belief system of war must be addressed because it is so deeply indoctrinated in your young men. Mothers of young boys, you must step away from violent toys or any talk of war. You must show them how to be strong and to develop their bodies by lifting and playing and climbing and jumping. These are the ways to manhood. Do not teach them to be violent. There is a natural response in the ego mind that will keep you safe, that will use the body that is honed if it is required. It does not need to be a focus.

Mothers of little girls, do not teach your daughters to be passive. Teach them about their bodies and how they work and the power of their creative force that lives in each of them. Teach them to respect and love themselves and to insist that others respect and love them as well. Do not allow them to be demeaned or used or put in second place in any circumstance. Teach all your children self-respect. Teach all your children to honor and love and utilize their bodies to their full capacity, and you will bring into being a society of equality.

Our societies are equal. They were long in the making. You are stumbling out of a dark age and into a bright light that will be a very big challenge for you. We bring these messages forth with love in our hearts, honoring your journey. You have had a difficult time of it. You have had a difficult ride, and it is with great respect and joy that we come to visit your planet and offer our assistance as you wake up from the darkness that has enfolded your hearts and minds for such a long, long time.

# CHAPTER 25

# Help to Create a New Era of Cooperation

*Ananda and the Zetas*

We are Ananda. These sources of information are very import-ant for your planet over the next little while, so we want to get this information out. Enough beings are following this to turn the planet around, but that is not what you are taught in your society. You are not taught that a few thousand people can shift the con-sciousness of an entire planetary system, but when they are all aligned, when they have done their spiritual work and are focusing on that which is love, they can work miracles. Of course, that is what your beloved text [*A Course in Miracles*] and these books are all about, leading people down the pathway toward love and light.

Now, you have been deemed to be alone in this universe, and even those of you who are convinced that there is extraterrestrial life out there are not that happy when you come into contact with it, and that is why you have had to wait so long to bring these messages through. They are coming fast now. When a door opens in human consciousness, beings of higher mind will take full advantage of that — not in the sense you understand it to be, but because they know human minds can close again. Because of your belief structures and your fears, you can step back into the darkness. So there will be a great rush of information coming through a mind that is willing to open to these messages, and that is what is hap-pening here.

We are also bringing through all these disparate voices because it is important to understand that there are many, many races of extraterrestrial beings who wish to make contact with your planet. There is not just one type. That is another prejudice you have on your planet, this belief that there is only one type of extraterrestrial being.

So once again we pass you to another collaborative component in the Earth rescue mission. That is how we look at it, and that is how they look at it. There is a time coming very rapidly when it is imperative for more people to have this information because the shifts and changes that your planet will go through will be assisted by every person who is fearless and defenseless and who understands the magnitude of the events that are approaching your beautiful planet.

✳      ✳      ✳

[Note: This transmission had a very different feel to it. The consciousness I channeled was almost childlike with a very innocent feel and movements of hands and fingers that would be akin to a five-year-old's. It had a very sweet and gentle demeanor. I enjoyed this exchange very much.]

Species are all different. We are different from the oncs you have been speaking to up to this point. We are much smaller, and we are "classic alien" looking: We are very thin, and we have large heads and big eyes. We are less emotional than you are. We are not here as teachers; we are here as facilitators doing work. We will be some of the beings you encounter once communication/contact has been made with the higher-realm consciousness beings. You will need lots of boots on the ground, as you say, but we are not soldiers. We are workers. We are workers who will assist you in the physical application of some of these scientific technologies that will help clean your waters.

We see your waters are very polluted at this time, and this is something we are excited to help you with. We want you to be able to drink your lake and river waters. That is how they should be. At one time on your planet, that is how they were. We were helpers then too. In your history, there were great civilizations on your planet that were in constant contact with extraterrestrial adventurers and ambassadors.

## Telepathic Messages of Peace

We always work as helpers. That is our path, our destiny. We are not leaders. We will be in the trenches with you, moving dirt and water and rocks around. That is what we are good at. Every revolution needs beings who are willing to put their shoulders to the wheel and to help bring forth the constructions, the water transportation systems, the food-manufacturing systems, and the nurturing systems that will benefit your planet.

We are happy to be assigned this job. We are not ambitious, and we do not have the desire to be special. We know that the truth and the reality of accomplishment are wonderful things, so we do not put on fancy garb or crowns or act as leaders. We will be those beings you see working hard toward the reclamation of your soils and your air, and these sorts of things. There is so much work to do on your planet that you have no idea how to deal with it. You keep belching forth pollution because of your training and your rulers. You keep destroying this most beautiful library of genetic material that you call Earth.

We do not call your planet Earth. We call it the Blue Planet and sometimes the Green Planet, depending on the season when we show up. It is with great love that we come to you now and offer our services. The stories about extraterrestrials who abuse, manipulate, and masquerade are not stories about us, but because of our appearance, you might think those stories are about us. You will always know us by the feeling you get when we show up. If you see a small being with thin arms and legs and a large head with big eyes and you don't like how you feel, ask them to leave. That will not be us.

When you encounter us, we will send telepathic messages of love and peace to your mind. You will know that you are safe, and you will feel acceptance, kindness, and peace. You will have an ecstatic feeling, a little flutter in the heart, a little increase in breath that is excitement, or anticipation of contact. That is how you will know it is us.

If you feel oppressed or constricted in your movements in any way that someone is doing or thinking about doing or saying something to you that is unloving or unwanted, that is not us. We would never impinge on your perfectly authentic free will. We are here only to assist, only to bring to you the arms and legs and understanding and abilities that your planet needs to move through the cleansing process and the revolution you are participating in at this time.

We are here, but we are out of phase in your skies when we monitor you. Because your scientific understanding is limited, you do not understand that there are frequencies in which we reside that are just out of visual range for your human eyes. We are waiting for you to decide to heal your planet. We are merely a turn away on a dial. (We use the language you understand here.) We do not use dials in that sense. We use thought manipulation to control our vehicles, and that is what you will encounter with us. You will encounter our thoughts, and you will know our deepest wish is to heal your planet and to heal your minds.

These messages come from a place of love. These messages come from a place of connection to your hearts as brothers and sisters. We look very different from you, and we know that some of you will be frightened when you first see us because of the movies and the stories about alien beings, but we are not aliens. We are lovely beings who have only your best interests as our wishes, but we cannot force you into any kind of compliance because we are good, we are kind, and we are sweet. The beings who will force you, cheat you, and manipulate you will always bring up a feeling of negativity, and you witness this on your planet at this time.

### Pay Attention to How You Feel

You look at your governments and feel negativity because you know they are not taking you where you need to go. You must take you where you need to go. You must become free. You must go into your hearts and minds and align with what you want. Invite us in. We cannot come without your invitation. We are not allowed to because we function in all realms that require us to honor and love all beings and all life. Other reptilian overlords do not feel this way. They function in lower frequencies, and that means they will override you with their power. They will manipulate you to take your free will from you and use it against you.

You are all choosing what you are choosing. You actually own your free will, but they have tricked you. They have miseducated you and lied to you. They put pretty faces on darkness. That is their way of getting you to use your free will against yourselves.

We will never do that to you. We will only bring feelings of caring and nurturing when you meet us. Know that when you encounter us (which you all will in the next 100 years), that is how you tell a good extraterrestrial from a negative extraterrestrial. You know by how it makes you feel.

You will also know, by how you feel, whether you are in alignment with the higher frequencies of the structures of mind that the beings coming to your planet hold. If you are not in alignment with them, then you will feel bad. If you are in alignment with truth and love, you will feel good. These are the endless truths repeated time and again throughout history from every being that comes to talk to you. We all bring the same message. We have evolved out of war, and we bring you only the truth. We bring you only our help, and we ask you to share your hopes and dreams and wishes with us as you come into this new era of cooperation and action.

We are what you think of as the little grays, but we are not the mechanical and unloving Grays. We are the beautiful and sweet and kind Zetas that will assist you in your labors.

# CHAPTER 26

# Embrace the Change

*The Ashtar Command*

C ompliments on your work so far! This is Ashtar, leader of the outpost known as Saphasta. This is not a name you know. Saphasta is a location outside your solar system, and we are based there. Ashtar is a name you know. I am a leader, a collaborator with the Galactic Federation aspects that work with your planet. It is important for you to realize that a great orchestration is happening in space. A great deal of preparation has been going on in space, ongoing attempts to peacefully contact your governing bodies, but they have become contaminated to such a degree that there is a concerted effort to overthrow the rulers of your planet.

That was what your 2012 shift in energy was all about. The "hands off" policy was removed in 2012 because of the cyclical nature of your planet's journey through the universe. So there are times of ebb and flow, just as there are tides coming in and out, and just as there are seasons changing and shifting, regardless of what you do. So too are there energetic shifts that your planet goes through, and it has just ended one cycle and is entering a new cycle, one that is of a higher frequency and will insist on transformation and the relinquishment of negative controls by your society's leadership. The leadership has become highly contaminated, but a revolution is afoot now.

You see structures being reassigned and reconfigured, but your training in school — keep everything the same, study the same languages, have routines, line up, be good, don't step in disorder — is done for a reason. These training programs make change very, very frightening for you as a society, but there is a generation of youngsters coming up who will not conform. They were born to be revolutionaries. They were born to rattle the cages of all of you who are staid and secure in your routines and your habits and your material possessions — your jobs, your mortgages, and all these things. These are not realities from Spirit's point of view. These are prisons from Spirit's point of view.

We are extraterrestrial beings who have a vigorous spiritual life. That is how we have mastered the universe, telepathic communication, and traveling through time and space in an inordinately swift and efficient way. You, in the mean time, are bumbling around on your planet in gas-guzzling cars. Do not compare yourselves to us. Do not think that we are less than you; on the contrary, we are here to help you evolve. We come with a little arrogance — yes, indeed, you can hear it in my voice — but that is because you are very arrogant and want to keep things the way they are. You do not know what you are asking for. You do not know how limited your vision is.

Some kindergarten children do not want to graduate into the next class because they like the blocks and the crayons they are playing with. They do not realize they have full and exciting lives coming their way. Children do not like that change, and you are like children in your evolutionary journey. We are your teachers, the beings who will assist you in expanding your horizons physically, mentally, emotionally, and spiritually. You have very limited minds compared to what you can have.

You are all capable of direct conscious contact with us. You are all capable of having constant and loving guidance to help you on your way. Trust us, if you tuned in to us every day and asked us what we would do, it would not look like the things you are doing. You would not be at war. You would not judge. You would not eat bad food, and you would not think bad thoughts. All these things keep you in this slow, heavy, materialistic prison in which you find yourselves.

## Stop Doing Things You Don't Enjoy

Many of you are breaking out. You are taking yoga, going on expeditions, and being creative, but still the training and conditioning of your society holds you prisoner. It is time to bust out of this limited thinking. We throw down a gauntlet, here and now, to challenge you to stop doing what you always do.

Break your habits! Get up, and do something different! Meet people, take a class, go to a different country, or sell your car to buy something more fuel-efficient. Learn something new. Do something different. If you have a job and a mortgage you hate or a life that you hate but keep doing, ask yourself why you live your life this way. Why are you doing something you do not want to do? At the end of your life, you will see it all as wasted time. There is no God wanting you to suffer and sacrifice yourselves; there is only the voice in your head, the fictitious voice of God put there by your limiting religious beliefs. Yes, we understand that they were indoctrinated in violent and punishing fashion, but it is time to take back your free will. It is time now for you to say, "What do I want to do this year? I want to do something different. I can feel it in my bones." This is the year you must do that.

Time is running out for your planet, and there will be massive shifts and changes coming. If you are stuck in routines, attached to your financial security and thinking your home is your life's investment, you will be sorely tested. So challenge those beliefs now. Challenge those limiting thoughts and ideas now, and you will fare much better as the changes come across your planet. All the beings in this book are here to tell you your planet is going to change, your culture is going to change, your climate is going to change, and your celestial positioning is going to change.

You will sign up with the Galactic Federation once you have evolved enough to receive privilege in that council. We do not let just anyone in there, and the way you are functioning now — fighting each other, attacking each other, polluting your planet, and all of these things that show your ignorance and lack of education — suggests you do not deserve to be on that council.

We know that you are educated and kept ignorant by the powers that be, but each of you has the power of a god. Each of you has free will, and now is the time to assert it. You must say, "I no longer wish to do this. How can I change?" If people depend on you, get them in a group, and say, "I am no longer going to do this. What shall we do? We must work as a team" (a family, a group, or a collaborative community — whatever it is). If you do not want to do something anymore, then it is your responsibility to live a life that is full of your passion, your desire, your wants, and your destiny. That is what will bring you out of this confined and limiting thought structure that you call your society.

## Do Something Different

If you could see the freedoms, the pleasures, the interest, and the adventures that are potentials for your planet, you would look up from your boredom and your mesmerizing televisions and say, "Count me in! I am going on this adventure." But you do not know enough to do that, so we are here to tell you: Set yourself free in your mind first. It is in your mind that your behavior arises, and it is there that you must begin the journey.

If you are afraid to speak and to act, do nothing! Go inside your mind and ask yourself, "What can I do to free my mind? Should I look at the subjects I'm interested in instead of medicating myself with mindless television? Should I investigate places to live that I would prefer rather than seeing myself stuck in this 'prison'?" These are creative juices and energies that will bring opportunities and more information. If you begin to align with what you desire to experience, it will manifest! It will come to you. It will not come to you if you recite a litany of reasons it will not come to you. You empower those when you do that.

So become braver, more outspoken, and more loving. Do not become outspoken in attacking people; become outspoken about the things you value. Speak of the law you would like to see enacted on your planet. Speak about the environmental shifts and changes you would like to see.

Do not attack the polluters active now, but ask yourself whether you are polluting. Are you doing something that is not helping the planet? Change that, and be happy that you are changing it. Don't do it as a sacrifice, and don't do it like a martyr. Do it with joy and strength and purpose.

Get up each day, and live your life as if it is yours alone, because that is the truth of the matter. Your life is yours alone, and it contributes to the world. So live your life passionately and happily, and express who you are, the unique you who is strange and weird and nonconformist. That is what your planet needs. It does not need more people to behave by going off to their jobs with their heads down as they trudge through their misery. It needs people who get up and say, "I am going to paint a picture today! I am going to go on a daylong hike today. I am going to dream today. I am going to help somebody today." The world does not need more hamsters running on wheels. That is not working for your planet. Take a good look around to see what this belief system has created.

The revolutionaries are at work. They are dismantling your system, fed by the higher frequencies that are coming to your planet, and they are going to continue increasing. Jump on this train! It is moving fast now. Don't get left behind at the station. Don't be one who says, "They told me I would need to do this, but it is too late now." Get onboard! Be healthy, fit, strong, happy, excited, passionate, and joyful! Be the one who people look at and say, "What happened to that person? He (or she) used to be like me, and now he (or she) is happy and vibrant and living an exciting life. I want a little bit of what he (or she) has." Be the inspiration for the beings around you. Do not conform to the dark and joyless world that you have been trained for.

We await your presence. We look forward to engaging with happy, creative, and expressive humans. It is nothing but a joy to meet humans like that, and we have met a few. Many of you have traveled through space, encountered our ships, and held conversations with us. Humans who are free are nothing but a joy. Become one of those humans. Step up now, today, and do something different. Do something that engages your passions, your physical energy, and your sexual energy, even (if you are very brave), and become more alive.

It is with great joy that we join in this treatise, and we want you to know that there is great love and support for you. We gave you a little talking to here to get you motivated, to get you going, and to get you up in arms — not arms of war, but arms of love.

Hug each other, love each other, create, be free, and know that everything is going to be okay. Your planet is breaking free from years of oppression. It is going to transform into a lightbody, and it will need you to be lightbodies yourselves. So begin the process today of lightening up. Lighten up your mood, lighten up your food, and lighten up your perspective on the world. We thank you, and we will be in communication again.

# CHAPTER 27

# Know That You Are Powerful

*The Arcturian Council*

We are the Arcturian Council, and we have been channeling through many beings on your planet at this time. This is a difficult time for humanity, and we are bringing forth information to help you understand yourselves. This is our purpose. We come from Arcturus, and we have been here for a very long time. This is not a new adventure for us. We have spoken to many beings on your planet throughout history, especially mystics and people who meditate. We often assume the voice of God for them not because we are pretending to be God but because that was the only voice they would allow in their consciousnesses. So some of the loving messages your saints and enlightened ones have brought forth have been from us.

The Arcturian Council is a group of beings from our star system. A star system can have many inhabited planets; hence, we have a council that represents all the communities and constellations within our star system. Why are we here? Why do we care about you? Well, everything is connected in this universe. Every single thing is connected, and particular star systems are connected with each other more strongly than others. The Arcturian star system is very connected to Earth.

We have a strong interrelationship with you, and we benefit from doing spiritual counseling and teaching work with humanity, just as a Westerner might go to a remote village and perhaps take in some alternative medicine or visit medical practitioners or look into some education.

This is the kind of connection we have with you. Westerners might say, "Why would you go to some remote village in Africa to help people?" Those people are inspired to do that from Spirit. It is part of their karmic journey to self-understanding and self-realization, and different civilizations have this relationship with you. That is why so many of us are showing up now.

Earth is going through a great battle for freedom, and it is an intentional battle. You must take back your free will and your intention to live in a loving way, and we are bringing information forth so that you understand how to win that battle.

We cannot do it for you, but we can help point you in the right direction, as can all other extraterrestrial beings who are amassing around your planet to intentionally attract to you, as a society, love and freedom. This is what you must seek for yourselves. You must seek love and freedom in whatever way you can.

We understand that this being is channeling very loving material. We have joined in this conversation because the frequency is the same. There are many disparate groups of extraterrestrials who hold the same frequency, just as there are lower-frequency groups who hold the same frequency. Not all the lower-frequency extraterrestrials who have contaminated your society are from the same place, but they hold the same frequency. So for all intents and purposes, they have the same effect on you. The same thing is happening in the higher-frequency extraterrestrials.

We have a peaceful society that is dedicated to the expansion of consciousness through the practices of love, and we bring forth a frequency that is healing to the minds of those of you who have been trampled on. We bring a frequency that is supportive, so whenever you encounter us, you will feel good. You will feel loved, and you will feel invisible caring arms around you. This is not what you will feel when you encounter the lower-frequency extraterrestrials. They might visit you in your nighttime and cause nightmares or feelings of terror, paralysis, wishing to speak but being unable to, negativity, or circular thinking about particular issues, causing stress in the body.

None of us in the higher realms will cause those feelings in you. You will always feel an elevation. You will always feel inspiration, anticipation, and enthusiasm for what we are saying, knowing that it is in alignment with the deeper truths of your spiritual being and your nature. This is what you must identify with, and we want to join in this collaborative conversation because only in your hearts and minds can this battle be won.

Physical altercations happen between higher-frequency extraterrestrials and lower-frequency extraterrestrials within your physical 3D reality, but that is not how this battle will be won. This battle will be won in your hearts and minds because that is where all our power and strength comes from. It comes from our alignment with love and truth and freedom. These are all words for the same thing: Freedom comes from loving and following the truth, truth gives you freedom, and truth allows you to love. They are all interchangeable and interconnected in that sense.

Your planet looks so controlled because taking away freedom means you have difficulty finding the truth, and if you cannot find the truth, you're not able to love. And that is why your world is such a mess: Your freedoms and your access to truth have been limited, so your ability to love has been compromised.

## Do Things You Love

Your ability to love will return the keys to the door to freedom. Love will open the gateways to truth, but you must choose it. You must love yourselves first. Listen to how you feel, because your guidance comes from a place deep within you. This guidance will always be kind because it comes from your true self. If it ever seems unloving or hateful, the guidance is not coming from your true self, so do not listen to it.

You cannot make sound decisions with a mind that is deeply contaminated and confused. The mind-training programs that this being is offering are on the path to mastering these three realms. And we support that process here.

We do not follow that exact process because we live on a planet where wisdom has reigned for a very long time, truth rules, and love is given free expression. So we have established our own principles and practices. We will be very happy to share those principles and practices with you when we get to make conscious, direct physical contact with humanity. For now you must work within the systems provided for you because they have been designed for you to work within this prison-planet place.

So use the means that have been given to you. Listen to the voice that is coming through this being because it is designed to speak to you where you are. It is not coming from a place of "better than," and it is not coming from a place of "different from." It is designed specifically to use the roots and routines and beliefs you hold now to give you more freedom.

You must seek truth, freedom, and love as your purpose. Your minds are contaminated by the belief that when you have the perfect career and you are successful and rich, things will change. They will not change. Those beliefs about success and wealth come from within the system and are designed to keep you away from spiritual practice. They are designed to keep you on the treadmill of seeking financial security, preoccupied decade after decade in your incarnation until you are so worn out and disillusioned that you give up. That means your life is wasted, and you don't make the shift in consciousness that is required to move through your evolution.

What we see are beings who are so distracted by materialism and money that they step away from spiritual practice. Even those who are engaged in spiritual practice put big boundaries on it so that it doesn't interfere with their financial security or their material wealth.

That will be the change that is the biggest challenge for you in coming years. As the planet goes through her evolutionary shift, the systems that are on the surface, in her, and surrounding her will have to match her frequency to survive. So our advice to you in seeking truth, freedom, and love is to make sure you work at something you love. Even if you cannot do it full time, do it during evenings and on weekends. Plant the seeds of that which you would like to work in that is love based. For example, if you are an accountant and you hate your job and want to be a healer, spend some of that hard-earned cash. Don't put it in the bank; invest it in freeing yourself from the constraints of a structure you don't want to be in anymore. This is not self-centered. It is loving to the planet because these old systems that train you to stay in what you hate keep the frequency of the planet down and prevent the evolutionary shifts in small increments.

## Embrace the Desire to Break Free

Evolutionary shifts will happen now, but they are going to happen in big increments because no pressure has been released. Think of an earthquake fault line. Many small earthquakes might prevent a big earthquake. Well, in your society, because of your training and the dampening of your spiritual nature into materialism, you have not been making the small evolutionary shifts that you need to make. But there is a wave of transformation afoot on your planet that is now irresistible, so those of you deeply indoctrinated in compromise or sacrifice or martyrdom or suffering will experience a tremendous desire to break free, and we want you to know that this is the most important step you can take.

This desire to break free is not erroneous or delusional. It is the true and natural alignment with your inner spiritual nature. Wild animals will die if you lock them up in cages, but domesticated animals can tolerate that because they have been genetically engineered to. That is what has happened to you. You have been genetically engineered to tolerate imprisonment, suffering, and lack of freedom.

Override your genetic programming, and connect with the spiritual motivation within. These are two different things. Your physical body has a tendency to do certain things. You have a tendency to talk. You have a tendency to walk upright. You have a tendency to move your arms and legs. You have a tendency to eat, and you have a tendency to procreate. But your spirit can override those things.

Your spirit can put you on a fast or an exercise program, and your spirit can get you to quit your job. These are things that are very, very important for you to understand. The tendencies of the physical structure can be overridden. They are less powerful than the spirit and the directed, focused mind.

This is what we want you to understand. Know that you are powerful and can override your programming. You are powerful and can override the conditioning and the training of your society. It is imperative now, in whatever small way you can, to call in higher-frequency beings through the practice of higher-frequency thoughts and behavior. Do not call in anyone if you are fearful and judgmental and hate-filled and feeling terrible. Get yourself to feel better first. Do things that are kind to yourself by following your interests, exercising the body, and eating well.

When you get to a better space, call out for beings of light and love only. You must use these words. "Only beings of light and love are welcome in my consciousness, and any other being of low frequency, get away from me! Get out of my physical structure. Get out of my family, and get out of my home. You are not welcome. Get out of here. I seek only love and light." In using words such as these, you banish, with your free will, power that is not welcome. Lower-frequency beings are only allowed to reside within you when you are in a maudlin, depressed, weakened state through your conditioning and physical tendencies.

When you use the spiritual power that is your right, lower-frequency beings will leave you alone, and you will have contact with only higher-frequency consciousness (in many different forms, of course). We are here to let you know there are many different forms. There are the pure, nonphysical beings, such as the ones who guide this channel; there are extraterrestrial beings who have advanced spiritual evolution but are still within your space-time reality; and there are beings who exist in other realities. So there are many forms of consciousness that will be able to access you once this planet's prison bars have been removed.

Make sure that you are on the path of love, freedom, and truth. When you are on the path of love, freedom, and truth, you do not need to fear or close yourself off from communication or Spirit. When you are on the path to love, freedom, and truth, you will bump into all the people and messages and inspirations that you need to guide you on the correct path toward your destiny. Your destiny is one of love, truth, and freedom. Our destiny is one of love, truth, and freedom, and we are here to help any population that has been separated from love, truth, and freedom through duplicitous means. You are among those people.

So know that we come in love and friendship, and we come with love, truth, and freedom as our guides to teach you how to have love, truth, and freedom as your guidance system. We are the Arcturian Council, and we will speak to you again soon.

# CHAPTER 28

# Earth Has Extraordinary Support

*The Andromedan Council*

These are the greatest days of your planet's life. You have heard many stories in the past few chapters from differing members of the Galactic Federation. We are coming together here to show support for planet Earth. We are coming together to help you, but you must ask us. It is the greatest law of the universe. Free will is yours, and we can only respond to your call. We want you to know there is great love for Earth and all the beings on her who have been led astray. You have been taken deep into the darkness, and you have become lost and confused not through any fault of your own but through manipulations on many levels. We have talked about what has been done to you, and now we want to talk about what will happen to you when you are free.

## Let Your Heart Lead You

We all come with beautiful cultural stories of overcoming the darkness and of walking into freedom and love together, and as our cultures evolved, we became members of the Galactic Federation. That is what we want for you. We want to offer you a seat on the board of the Galactic Federation, but it must come from a planet that is united in its vision of what truth, freedom, and love are. You must agree that you want to participate in a society that is loving and kind in focus. You must agree that you want to help each other achieve the basic necessities of life. You must agree that the overabundance of wealth in one person's hands is unnecessary, that a certain level of wealth is enough for anyone, and that once that level is reached, the extra can be shared. This is a basic principle of a social system that works.

You are encouraged in your individuality and your creativity and your desires to improve yourself, but at a certain level of accomplishment when you have become wealthy, those extra rewards get turned over to society to help bring others up to the level you are at. This is love demonstrated.

Rampant capitalism is not loving. It is destructive to your societies and to your planet. When one human being has millions of dollars in the bank and walks past starving people, that is not love. That is not sanity. It is craziness and hatred. It is very, very unloving indeed, and we wonder at it.

You have had many teachers come to your society, but because of the manipulations of the teachers and teachings, the lessons have been distorted into nonsense. The lessons have been distorted into lies, and as a society, you are following the wrong leaders. Your heart must be your leader. You must know that when you feel good, you are doing something right; when you are kind, you are doing something right; and when you are loving, you are doing something right. But in a society that is very, very distorted, each person becomes so confused that bad feels good and wrong feels right.

## Capitalism Is Not the Answer

Your world focuses on capitalism. It is a vision that has contaminated the minds of all the beings on this planet, and it is a very narrow view of reality. In our system and in the Galactic Federation, the welfare of all is kept front and center in our actions. Trust us, if we had not valued you as a species, we would have come in and transformed your world much as the current rulers did. They did not care for you. They have bullied you and distorted your experiences and taken from you the ability to truly understand through a natural growth cycle. Their time is done now, but their teachings are strong in your minds, and we must remind you of this as you come to the next phase of your civilization's development.

We must remind you that your fears have been purposely implanted and cultivated, so your beliefs about money constantly rise to the surface of your minds even though there are many societies and civilizations of high frequency that do not possess this thing called money. Money is not required. Over time, your society will evolve to a moneyless system. This does not mean a digital money society, as some of the globalists want you to believe. A society where you are not supported, encouraged, and given everything that is available to you as a resource is not a moneyless society. When you are kept isolated, having to support yourself only and to look after yourself only, then money works. It works to keep you away from each other.

In your society, you have been trained to hoard your money, keep it secret, not speak about it, not share it, and save it for a rainy day. These are capitalistic views that are destroying you. We come as a collective now, telling you that capitalism is not going to be the system used in the new world. We are not speaking about the new world order here. We must be careful about our language because you have nasty stories about the new world order, and you should be afraid of that.

The New Earth that is arising, this loving place, will be supported in an integrated fashion from many different kinds of resources. You will support each other, and we will support you. We will assist you with technologies so that you don't have to work hard to pay your electric bills and for your gasoline-powered vehicles. The energy systems will be free. We will bring in technologies that will allow you to clean up your planet and produce more food. These are some things we will offer you.

In exchange for those teachings and resources, we will ask you to become kinder, more generous, more forgiving, and more loving. It will be a mutually beneficial system. We come as teachers. Just as teachers teach small children how to write and are very patient and do not necessarily expect the children to pay them back in like form, we do not expect you to pay us back in like form.

Part of the capitalistic mindset is that you must always pay someone back or that you owe a person who helps you. This is a very unevolved state of consciousness, and we want you to realize this as we go into this next phase because that is what the enemies of your freedom will tell you. They will tell you that if you work with the Galactic Federation and the Andromedan Council, you will owe us. That is the ego's way, the capitalistic way. That is not how we view the coming transaction. We know that to give and receive are one. What we give to you, we benefit from in physical, spiritual, and energetic terms.

As we conclude this dialogue with you, we want you to know that there will be many more conversations such as this. This being is open to having an ongoing conversation with many aspects of the Galactic Federation, and she will be asked to work on that assignment. For now, her assignment with us is over.

We bring you a message of future benefit and of impending expansion, and we want you to know that there are beings outside your vision and knowledge at this time who support you with love and kindness and an integrity that you are not very familiar with. Your society has been cruel, viciously violent, and manipulative. We are none of those things, but you are trained in those things. So you must begin to heal your hearts and minds and open to the possibility that there are beings who are generous and loving out in the universe.

## Leave Your Prison Cell

The history of your planet, as you have seen it in the past few thousand years has been terribly violent and sad. When we look at your world, we hold our hearts and wish you well, but we know that you cannot do it alone because you have been poisoned inside and out. Your Earth is poisoned, your minds are poisoned, and your hearts are poisoned. You are fearful beings, and you are smaller than you should be. You have the abilities to connect with us and create and love and expand far beyond your understanding at this point. You have been kept in solitary confinement, really, but the rescuers are coming. We cannot rescue you in the sense of freeing you from yourselves — you must do that — but we are here to offer you the means toward that end.

First, you must think about it. First, you must go inside and ask yourself whether you want to keep doing what you are doing. Do you want to keep living the way you are living? Do you want to keep kowtowing to the powers that be? Or would you rather seek freedom, health, and a cooperative society based on principles higher than capitalism?

We are the Andromedan council, and we are here to encourage you to ask these questions. Every one of you must ask these questions before you can change your mind. As long as you think you are the only beings in this universe, you are destined to be fearful and to stay locked in this mindset. But if you begin to question the status quo, if you begin to question the principles and ideas you have been indoctrinated with, then you will be able to ask that final question: "Am I willing to meet my galactic brothers and sisters openly and with a curious, if cautious, mind?" We understand that you will be cautious, but we want you to understand that there is a different way of life out here. We work together. We are distinct civilizations working together to bring expanded consciousness to different parts of the galaxy. It is your time now, and the vibration of your planet makes this inevitable, so you must ask yourself these questions.

The clock is ticking, and we ask you to consider this potential future. This potential future is better than the one you will get if you stay locked in fear and constriction as you have been taught. It is all you know. It is like a bird in an open cage, too frightened to leave. We are calling you into the expanse of space. We are calling you into the unlimited vista that is the true world. Your world has been and is still a prison for you. Most of you cannot imagine the potentials that exist and that we experience. So we ask you to contemplate this now. That is what it must be initially: a heartfelt inner journey of questioning what is.

It is time now for you all to look up from your small earthly lives at the stars, knowing you are starseeds, children of the universe, and we are all connected in love and compassion. We will communicate with you again at another point in time.

# CHAPTER 29

# Plant Seeds of Change

*Ananda*

There are secrets in your society that are global. Millions and millions of people are laboring under huge misconceptions that create negative emotion. The creative process on your planet has been usurped by beings who understand how creation works. As we have mentioned, what you think about with emotion is generated. So if you are deceived or manipulated and strong negative emotions are triggered, you will bring chaos into being. You will bring things that you do not want into being. This is exactly what has been and is being done to you day after day through your mass-media systems. This is marketing genius but also creative chaos.

You are being tricked into using your most powerful creative abilities to bring war, pollution, starvation, and the degradation of your society into being, and you are not aware of it because you are not aware of your tremendous creative abilities. You are a divine being. You have been given the abilities of a god because that is how God creates. God creates through endless creativity. That is the nature of God energy. God is not an individual being. God is an ever-extending force of love that holds things together and creates through love.

In a society such as yours that constantly promotes violence, hatred, judgment, self-loathing, superficial beliefs, materialism, and consumerism, this amazing power is distorted and diverted into systems that are not love based — for example, your beauty industry. Women are made to feel ugly, fat, too thin, or many other things through the systematic and constant bombardment of their minds with images of unreal beauty.

There is no teaching in your society of self-acceptance or the appreciation of inner beauty. There is no teaching in your society of true spirituality, which is self-honoring and self-loving. So half the people grow up in a state of negativity, wishing they looked differently than they do, wishing they could change their physical structures to conform to a completely artificial standard.

You have no idea of the energy that is wasted in this scenario. Time is wasted, and these people could be thinking much more valuable thoughts. The truth is, the creative force being sucked from half the population is enough to transform your world completely.

If every woman in your society were able to love and appreciate herself for her uniqueness and were encouraged from childhood to develop her skills and abilities with compassion, love, and kindness without the suffering and sacrifice that has been added as a distortion, you would see a completely different world. You would see a world where women are in positions of power. You would see a world where no children are sent to war, for no mother would send her children to war if she were raised in a loving way. This is one of the great losses of your society, and it is going to be one of the great revolutions that must take place in your world. It must begin with you. It must begin inside your heart and mind. When you look in the mirror, say, "I appreciate and love myself unconditionally, no matter what society says." This is a basic prayer every woman should say as she looks in the mirror.

"I appreciate and love myself unconditionally no matter what society says about how I should look or how I should be. I am designed exactly as I should be, and I am going to nurture all my interests, desires, and cares. I am going to investigate them and explore them and develop them."

If every woman on the planet had that instilled in her as a little girl, this world would be a different place. We are not blaming the women here! This is one of the control mechanisms that has been used in your society and has become a self-regulating system. Once you have indoctrinated a human mind with thousands of hours of negativity, it becomes the negative entity itself. It attracts negative experiences and creates negative relationships so that it is taken care of.

## Recognize Your Manipulation

Have you noticed how attacking all your television shows are? Many begin with an attack and a murder victim, and then they end with the retribution that comes through justice. The entire show is a play of hatred and retribution, and you watch these shows happily week after week. You go to your movie theaters and watch "heroes" mow down their enemies with machine guns, and you wonder why it happens in real life. You give your children video games that are hateful and murderous, and you wonder why they grow up and are unable to have loving relationships.

Your society is about to collapse, and we are here to help you go through that journey. It is unstoppable now because the society you have is not based on love. The society you have has been developed very carefully and cleverly, brick by brick, by people who have no love for you. It has been propagated and promulgated by people who do not care for the survival of your race or your planet.

You look around and see houses and roads and systems of governance and banking systems, and you think that is reality. It is not reality; it is a completely artificially created system of slavery and control. You look at nature and wonder at it. You envy the birds that fly around and pick up pieces of food here or there or catch a fish, and you think "Wow, what a wonderful world it would be if we could all just forage for our food or if we could live supported by nature."

Then again, some of you have big homes and fancy cars. You have figured out this system, but there is a hole inside of you, something missing, because you are taking from others. You are usurping the resources that should be shared among many for the few.

Some of you in the Western Hemisphere are very happy with the system you have. You have comfortable couches, big homes, fancy cars that go very fast, and all the money you need to buy all the things that you want. This world cannot survive this system. This world cannot live this way anymore because there are billions of people who are paying for that extravagant Western lifestyle.

The resources that are being taken from third-world countries in the form of minerals and gold and labor are supporting that system, but it is invisible to you. You think you deserve it. You think you are rich, but you are rich from a system that takes from half the world to give to the other half.

"Why," you ask, "is this system in place?" It is a system that is designed by beings who understand your consciousness, how human minds work. If you give people enough luxuries, they will stop asking questions. They will stop asking about the welfare of beings on the other side of the world. If you give them enough food, they will stop moving. If you give them enough television, they will stop thinking. If you give them enough training, they will behave themselves.

### The Transition to Freedom

From our point of view, you are a prison planet. You have been given a small cell in which to walk, to get a little bit of exercise. You get some pillows and a television in the corner, and you get fed regularly, but you are in a prison, indeed.

A prison release is about to happen. The guards are going to come along and open the doors to your cells, and they are going to say, "We are no longer bringing you your food, your television has been disconnected, and you are free to go." That is what is about to happen on your planet, and we are here to help prepare for that eventuality because for a while, you will sit within your cell and be confused and upset, and you will yell for the guard to bring you dinner, but they will not come. You must get out of the prison cell yourself. You must walk out into the daylight, and you will have to figure out how to live in freedom.

It will be a very difficult transition for your society — this walking out of the cell into freedom — because you have become dependent on the system. You have become constrained and limited. Your bodies are not strong, your minds are not strong, and your hearts are fearful. But that which you call God — that which you call nature, that which you call the benevolent force of love — will give you everything you need, and you will be given all the instruction you need to reclaim yourselves as you go through this process.

It will be a very big challenge for you all. Know to prepare for that event that the first steps are realizing it will happen and accepting it will happen. We tell you to turn your televisions off because they will be turned off. They will not be there forever, and if you are addicted to them, dependent on them, or want them more than anything, then you are going to be sorely challenged when those television sets no longer work.

Your food production systems will collapse because of climate change. If you have a lawn or a garden of any kind, we suggest you learn to grow your own food. In fact, we are not worried about you. We know that when you get hungry and there is no food in the stores, you will be very inventive and courageous. You will dig up your lawns or flowerbeds, regardless of the local bylaws, and you will begin to plant gardens.

You won't be able to plant if you don't have seeds or haven't prepared the soil, so do that now. Buy seeds, and make sure they are organic heritage seeds, not cloned or genetically modified seeds that you buy in your regular stores. Heritage seeds can be ordered from a seed catalogue to support unaltered strains of fruits and vegetables. You do not have to do it this minute or next week, but you will want to have seeds available in your freezer when you need them.

# CHAPTER 30

# Creation Perpetually Extends

*Ananda*

As we finish this book, we feel your fears and your concerns. We are out of time, and we understand that when you read words such as this, the ego becomes very fearful of death, change, and losing its possessions. We want you to know there is no divine retribution going on here. There is merely a balancing of energies. That is all that is happening.

The energies are out of balance as negativity has been fed over and over and good has been overridden by this perverse training system in which you find yourself. There has to be a righting of that energy. It is a natural thing. It is not because you are bad or evil, and it is not because God is angry with you. It is merely a natural balancing. Seasons come and go, and there seems to be death in the winter months, but the trees and plants grow again. This is the season you are coming to.

You are going to enter something like winter. It will seem as if everything is dying, and that is indeed the truth. As we have said many times throughout our teachings, only things that are supported and maintained with love can live for a long time. You all know that your society is not loving. You see its manifestations all around you. You see it in polluting cars, you see it in chastising parental training programs, you see it in corrosive and destructive cultural indoctrination programs, and you see it in punishing and limiting school systems. These are all unloving things, and they will not survive.

The universe is built on love, and this is what we must return to as we conclude this book. You must understand that love extends itself all the time in your world. It extends itself through the beautiful sunlight that provides life on your planet. It extends itself in the wind and in the waters that fall on beautiful Gaia's soils that nourish plants and trees that bear fruits and harvests for you to eat. It extends itself in creativity that arises in your mind as ideas and inspiration.

Love does not extend itself in war. It does not extend itself in limitation or hatred, nor does it extend itself in control or repression. Those are in the realm of the ego mind. The ego mind is fear based, limiting, and materialistic in nature. You, however, are not.

### Learn to Love Yourself

Your spirit is timeless, your spirit is limitless, and your spirit has access to all the information that has ever existed and that will exist in this universe. Your timeless spirit is exactly that — out of time. It is not bound by the rules of the ego, but if you believe in the ego, if you believe in time, and if you believe in death, then you will become fearful, and you will, indeed, become limited by those very laws. We are here to encourage you to expand your heart and mind out of the ego's realm. To do that, you must be retrained.

You have been severely trained in the ego's ways, and you are habituated to them. You think attacking other people will bring you what you want, separating from other people will keep you safe, and isolating and keeping your money to yourself will keep you secure. None of these things is true. They are all devices of the ego mind.

What will keep you safe is loving each other, opening to each other, and sharing the wealth and bounty of this planet with each other, and you will have to be retrained to do that. We have brought forth many books through this being to assist you on that journey.

A Course in Miracles is a basic mind-retraining program that we recommend to everyone. That book is divinely inspired, providing 365 lessons that take you deep within the structure of your psychology into the fundamental ways you create in this time and place that you call twenty-first-century Earth.

You have not been given the laws of creation; you have been given the laws of the ego, and they are not God's laws. They are not the loving laws of extension, love, caring, and compassion. They are the laws of money, restriction, violence, and control, but they are all you know. It is what you have been taught from the time you were babies. You were smacked when you were naughty and broke the rules. You were put in the corner and punished at school when you did not conform. Your parents glared at you when you brought home bad marks, and you have learned, year after year, to conform and behave. You have become too frightened to stand up to the powers that be and the controlling mechanisms in your society, and as we have said, you must be retrained.

The lessons of *A Course in Miracles* align your mind with love, and stop it from aligning with judgment, fear, and hatred. They stop you from aligning your mind with separation. This is a very disciplined practice, and not all of you will be able to accomplish this. Not all of you will be able to understand the language, so we have brought through many books to assist you in understanding the principles and foundations of your society and what has transpired through your complicit behavior. Yes, you have joined in this imprisoning process that you are seemingly a victim of. You are not a victim of it; you have been trained to volunteer for it.

The solution is to reeducate yourselves. You cannot continue to sit in front of televisions, being indoctrinated in this system, and expect to become free and strong. It cannot be done. You must turn your televisions off. You must stop watching the political charades. These political games are designed to upset you, anger you, and separate you from your brothers and sisters. Look around you. They are doing a very good job. You are upset, you are angry, and you are afraid.

We want you to focus on love exclusively. You must focus on transforming the frequency of your consciousness because the frequency of your consciousness is harvested like a source of energy, a mineral, from this Earth. Your frequency is being harvested to keep negative systems at play and in operation.

When you begin to turn your mind toward love, when you begin to act in a more loving way, and when you become gentler — first with yourself and, consequently, with others — you will begin to starve the system of the energy that it needs. This is a very difficult concept for you to understand as beings who have been taught in a secular education system and frightened away from spirituality by the brutality of the church and its history. We ask you to look up to the stars and open your hearts first to yourselves. Learn to love yourselves.

Some of you joined us early on in our teachings, and you believed they were just spiritual teachings, nondualistic teachings, that love is all there is. You came in with simplistic ideas about what this world is and what these teachings were all about. We want you to know that there is dualism and there is unity consciousness. Dualism is the world of the ego, dark and light, hatred and love, and black and white, what you know as the ordinary world. But there is another world, and it is the world of unity consciousness.

In the worlds of unity consciousness, where many of these lightbeings, these highly evolved extraterrestrial beings, come from, dualism has faded, and they have realized that everything is connected. Each mind in a society is joined to every other mind, and together they create the reality they experience as that society. If that society is focused on love, beings manifest systems, hierarchies, governmental agencies, and education systems that are loving. If the minds focus on hatred and fear and scarcity, they create the very same systems within society, and that is what you are manifesting in your dualistic world.

## Forgive

There is another way, and you must come at it from within. You must walk the path of love. The great forgiveness practice of your world is the Holocaust. You must forgive that and understand that the beings who participated in that horrific experience knew what they were doing before they came into physical form. They understood that they would have a particular experience, and they understood that if they had that particular experience, they would come to understand more deeply the errors of their thinking.

The victims came to understand that they did not need to be victims anymore, that they did not need to be weak anymore, and that they did not need to be taken advantage of anymore. The perpetrators understood that they did not need to be cruel anymore, that they did not need to hurt anymore, that they did not need to attack anymore, and they did not need to damage anymore. In that natural learning process, they came to see the errors of their ways. Each came to see his or her errors. One was not worse than the other.

To be a victim is no worse than to be a perpetrator. To be hurt is no worse than to hurt. From Spirit's point of view, that lesson was learned, and the individual beings who took part in that horrific experiment learned their lessons. But each of you who came afterward has been indoctrinated in your thinking, and you have kept that hateful experience alive, to your detriment.

When you keep an experience like that alive, intentionally indoctrinated in your minds over and over again with horrific images and stories and movies showing up at regular intervals so that you do not forget it, you bring that same energy into being again, because that is how creation works. Whatever you focus on, your get more of, whether you want it or not. If it is in your mind, it will come into being, and you must understand this as the reason for your forgiveness practice. If you do not understand this, you will not be able to forgive. You will tell that story over and over again, and you will remain a victim of that story. Whether you are a perpetrator or a victim does not matter. You will get to experience that horrible energy over and over again, so you must forgive it.

You must pray for those past enemies who you believe were evil but are not. They are merely playing out the dualistic game of hatred and fear and love on your planet. You must rise above the battlefield and become the one who sees there is a bigger game to play here. This is a very difficult thing to forgive in your society because of the training that you have had, but we want you to know that it is the only way you are going to bring peace to this place.

## People Have Been Manipulated through Religion

The space program secrets that your governments have been participating in are the other great reveal we bring to your minds. There has been a long association with extraterrestrial beings on your planet, and it has not been the best kind. In 2012, a line was drawn in the sand and crossed, and now we can bring through the truth of your world.

You have been manipulated for a very long time, and one of the devices used by these extraterrestrial beings was religion. Your religions have brought you into limiting and restrictive consciousness, and they have used violence and hatred as their methodology. They have stripped indigenous peoples of their culture and their religion and their beautiful hair, knowing exactly what they were doing as they did it. They understood how humanity works. They understood how consciousness works, and they systematically and repeatedly destroyed those societies that knew better from the ground up.

By relearning these back-to-basics principles of life, you will rise out of this society of hatred and war. It seems impossible when you look at your great cities and your massive populations with technological involvement, but it can be done.

It can be done with the right knowledge, and you are getting the right knowledge. You must begin from within your consciousness to step back from violence and the overuse of technology. Put your phones down, and turn your televisions off. Better yet, get them out of your houses. They are broadcasting frequencies that make you agitated and fearful. They are constantly contaminating your auras and your electromagnetic systems. We understand that many of you need them for work, but they are used for nefarious purposes to transform your energy systems. So turn them of when you can, and get out in nature when you can.

Read wisdom and loving texts when you can, and most of all, make loving connections with your fellow brothers and sisters, your families, your communities, your neighbors, your country, and of course, your enemies.

## Practice Loving Kindness

We hope that you have been able to come to the end of this text with a deeper understanding of the tremendously complicated history and design of your society. We want you to live more simply, we want you to understand that nature is your friend, and we want you to understand that your brothers and sisters are your beneficiaries. They are the ones with whom you are going to build this new world, and those brothers and sisters, of course, come from the stars. They will connect with you more and more as you raise your frequency away from fear and into the realms of compassion and kindness.

These higher-frequency extraterrestrial beings are not separate from you. They are in the dualistic, three-dimensional world along with you, but they have learned the rules of the game, just as your leaders have learned the rules of the game and know exactly what they are doing when they deceive and manipulate you.

These higher-frequency extraterrestrial beings have love as their motivation. They have risen above the battlefield, and they are here to help you learn about yourselves. So when you come to the end of this book, begin your practice of loving kindness and forgiveness for yourself first, then your brothers and sisters, and then your enemies.

You will not be able to forgive your enemies immediately because you have been trained not to do that. The fact is you have been trained to kill them. But eventually you will be able to look on all beings on the planet with love and wish them well, and that will herald in a new era when you can, indeed, become friends with your galactic brothers and sisters and when you will be smart enough and loving enough and kind enough to take their lessons to heart and to bring into being a new world that is more favorable to all beings on your planet.

You are going to witness a great change in the next few years on your world, and we want to prepare you for that, but to do that, you must put down the weapons inside your minds. We understand that most of you are not packing guns and knives, but some of you are. We want you to put down the words you use as weapons, the weapons of hateful thinking.

We want you to put down the weapons you see used in your entertainment. Stop going to these things and watching these things, and begin to promote life by planting your food. Plant your garden, plant flowers, and plant seeds of happiness and love in every relationship you can.

We are Ananda. We are your friends, we are your teachers, and we are your fellow travelers on this most magnificent journey through consciousness. We hope that this book has challenged you and expanded you, and we hope it has whet your appetite for even more information.

# About the Author

Tina Louise Spalding was raised in a family that often visited psychics, so she is no stranger to the nonphysical world. Her channeling journey began when she settled down for a nap on the summer solstice of 2012. That afternoon, powerful energies surged through her body, leading to ecstasy, bliss, and an altered state of consciousness that lasted for almost a month. The feelings finally drove her to take an automatic writing workshop, where she was first made aware of Ananda. She then began to write for this group of nonphysical teachers who have come to assist us in our waking process.

Tina began channeling Jesus in the summer of 2013, when he appeared in her book *Great Minds Speak to You*. It proved to be a great challenge not only to accept the assignment he offered her — writing his autobiography — but also face many of the fears that this unusual experience brought up. Tina has been asked to channel for Jesus on an ongoing basis. Check her website, ChannelingJesus.com, for public offerings of his teachings.

Tina speaks for Ananda as a full trance channel, offering teachings and personal readings for those who seek more happiness, fulfillment, and connection with Spirit. She has dedicated her life to writing and speaking for Ananda and other nonphysical beings, sharing their wisdom and spiritual knowledge.

## THROUGH TINA LOUISE SPALDING

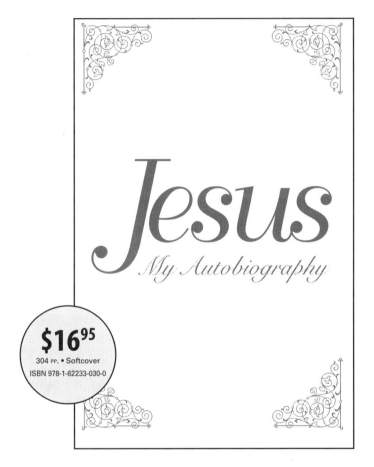

**$16⁹⁵**
304 PP. • Softcover
ISBN 978-1-62233-030-0

This insightful book is designed to free you from the limitations of your conditioned mind and to give you a better understanding of Jesus's life and teachings so that you can begin to transform your mind, your heart, and the world. Through Tina Louise Spalding, Jesus tells his story in his own words, clearing up misconceptions and untruths and describing his physical and nonphysical journeys that led to enlightenment.

## THROUGH TINA LOUISE SPALDING

# LOVE AND A MAP TO THE UNALTERED SOUL

*"True love is never-ending. It does not refuse or inflict punishment, it does not withdraw or have temper tantrums, and it does not punish. Love always is, and it always emits the same high frequency of absolute, unconditional caring and offering, of growing and creation."*
— *Ananda*

$16^{95}$ Softcover, 240 pp.
ISBN 978-1-62233-047-8

We think we know what love is, but in *Love and a Map to the Unaltered Soul*, we are challenged to broaden our definition and free ourselves from constraints we never realized we had. In these pages, you will learn that love is a process of climbing your ladder of consciousness. Through Tina Louise Spalding, the beings Ananda, Jesus, and Mary Magdalene give practical instruction and examples on how to find and keep love at the center of your life.

CHAPTERS INCLUDE

- The Unaltered Soul Seeks Experience
- Move beyond the Physical
- You Are Part of a Greater Oneness
- You Can Raise Your Frequency
- Seek Love Within
- You Create Your Experiences
- How to Find Love
- Align with Love to Find Happiness
- Question Your Beliefs
- Implement Healthy Routines
- The Choice Is Yours
- Forgiveness Demonstrates Love

## THROUGH TINA LOUISE SPALDING

# GREAT MINDS SPEAK TO YOU

With CD

"Many in spirit look on these times of difficulty, abundance, trouble, and innovation and wish to share with you their experiences and ideas. Some famous names and faces will come to mind as you read this book, and you will glean some fine information about their learning, their suffering, and indeed their experiences in the life after this life, for they all wish to tell you that there is no death as you perceive it to be. They are all there in their astral forms, enjoying their continued growth, their continued expansion, and their continued joy in living.

"Read this with an open mind and heart, and hear what these beings have to say. You have revered and reviled them in life; now let them complete their stories in what you call death, for that is the complete story. Is it not?"

— Ananda

$19⁹⁵ Softcover, 192 pp.
ISBN 978-1-62233-010-2

CHAPTERS INCLUDE
- Albert Einstein
- Jerry Garcia
- Ralph Waldo Emerson
- Marilyn Monroe
- John Huston
- Amy Winehouse
- Margaret Thatcher
- Princess Diana
- Susan B. Anthony
- Sylvia Plath
- Elizabeth Taylor
- John and Robert Kennedy
- Michael Jackson
- Cecil B. DeMille
- Jonas Salk
- Queen Mother Elizabeth
- George Bernard Shaw
- Pablo Picasso
- John Lennon

## THROUGH TINA LOUISE SPALDING

# MAKING LOVE TO GOD
## The Path to Divine Sex

"We have never seen more hurt and lonely people anywhere than on this planet at the moment. You are all in such a state that we have come from far and wide, from different times and places, to teach you how to relieve the deep suffering you are in. And indeed, it is in the bedroom, in your relationships to yourself, your lover, and God, that these hurts began.

"We are here to teach the way to divine bliss, and we know you are scared — scared to lie naked caressing your lover with rapt attention and honor. We know you are scared to kiss and connect, to feel such deep connection and pleasure that the ego starts to get very nervous, sensing the threat to the well-guarded and limited access to your heart that it deems to be safe.

"If we can turn the tide of thought in enough people, there will be a revolution of love on the planet, the likes of which you have never seen. Relationships will stabilize, marriages will last, and the passion and joy you so wish to experience will become manifest wherever you look."

— Ananda

**Making Love to GOD** — The Path to Divine Sex

Ananda through Tina Louise Spalding

**$19⁹⁵** Softcover, 416 PP.
ISBN 978-1-62233-009-6

**Topics Include**
- How We Came to Misunderstand Sexual Energy
- Using Divine Sex Energy
- Specific Steps and Sensations
- Blocks to Transformation
- A Transformed View of Sex and Sexual Energy
- Following the Path to Transformation
- Reaping the Harvest

## THROUGH TINA LOUISE SPALDING

# SPIRIT OF THE WESTERN WAY:
### Wake Up to Your Power —
### Heal the Collective Consciousness of the Western Mind

"Western civilization has been manipulated for a very, very long time into negative, low-frequency manifestations and structures of control, limitation, fear, and judgment. You cannot change this until you first see it, accept that it is so, and then, in awareness, shift your consciousness.

"These higher-frequency shifts and changes are difficult to attain unless you know what has been inflicted on you and what choices you are making and how they affect you. We bring you basic teachings about reality: what it is, where you come from, why you are here, what your body is, how you get sick, why you thrive, and more.

"This book is brought to you by many beings of high frequency who love you and your society very much. We have been assigned the spiritual practice to bring these teachings through this being so that we can help point you in the correct direction to find your way Home. We are Ananda. We are your friends, your teachers, and your fellow travelers on this most magnificent journey into consciousness."

— Ananda

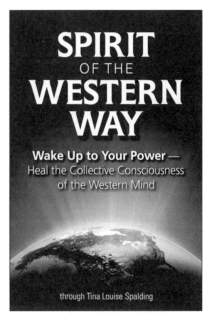

16.95 • Softcover • 176 PP.
ISBN 978-1-62233-051-5

CHAPTERS INCLUDE

- You Are Not Designed to See the Big Picture
- The Split Mind Cannot See Truth
- Nutrition for the Spiritually Minded
- Release Addictions to Find Freedom
- Books, Television, and Films as Nutrition for the Mind
- The Fallacies of Western Religious Thought
- Experience True Wealth and Freedom

♁ *Light Technology* PUBLISHING **Presents**

## BY TOM T. MOORE

# THE GENTLE WAY
### A SELF-HELP GUIDE FOR THOSE WHO BELIEVE IN ANGELS

"This book is for people of all faiths and beliefs with the only requirement being a basic belief in angels. It will put you back in touch with your guardian angel or strengthen and expand the connection that you may already have. How can I promise these benefits? Because I have been using these concepts for over ten years and I can report these successes from direct knowledge and experience. But this is a self-help guide, so that means it requires your active participation."  — Tom T. Moore

**$14.**⁹⁵ • 160 PP., SOFTCOVER • ISBN 978-1-891824-60-9

# THE GENTLE WAY II
### BENEVOLENT OUTCOMES: THE STORY CONTINUES

You'll be amazed at how easy it is to be in touch with guardian angels and how much assistance you can receive simply by asking. This inspirational self-help book, written for all faiths and beliefs, explains how there is a more benevolent world that we can access and how we can achieve this.

This unique and incredibly simple technique assists you in manifesting your goals easily and effortlessly for the first time. It works quickly, sometimes with immediate results, and no affirmations, written intentions, or changes in behavior are needed. You don't even have to believe in it for it to work!

**$16.**⁹⁵ • 320 PP., SOFTCOVER • ISBN 978-1-891824-80-7

# THE GENTLE WAY III
### MASTER YOUR LIFE

"Almost three years have passed since *The Gentle Way II* was published. Yet as many success stories as that book contained, I have continued to receive truly unique stories from people all over the world requesting most benevolent outcomes and asking for benevolent prayers for their families, friends, other people, and other beings. It just proves that there are no limits to this modality, which is becoming a gentle movement as people discover how much better their lives are with these simple yet powerful requests."  — Tom T. Moore

**$16.**⁹⁵ • 352 PP., SOFTCOVER • ISBN 978-1-62233-005-8

# ☥ *Light Technology* PUBLISHING *Presents*

TO ORDER PRINT BOOKS
Visit LightTechnology.com, Call 928-526-1345 or 1-800-450-0985,
or Check Amazon.com or Your Favorite Bookstore

## BOOKS THROUGH ROBERT SHAPIRO

## Are You a Walk-In?
### Book 19

**ARE YOU A WALK-IN?**

A NEW FORM OF BENEVOLENT BIRTH IS NOW AVAILABLE ON EARTH

Zoosh, Isis, Reveals the Mysteries, and More through **Robert Shapiro**

From the walk-in's perspective, the benefit of this new form of birth is coming into an adult body and being able to bring one's gifts to humanity without having to take the time to go through the usual birth process. The other side of this is that the walk-in has to resolve the physical, emotional, and spiritual issues that the walk-out left behind in order to completely express its own personality.

"This book is intended to be practical advice for day-to-day living for people who know they are walk-ins, for people who believe they might be walk-ins, or for the family and friends and business associates of people who are believed to be walk-ins. In short, this book is intended to serve the community to understand the walk-in phenomenon and for those who are experiencing it personally to be able to apply it in such a way as they are able to live easier, more comfortable, more useful, and more fulfilling lives."

— Reveals the Mysteries

$19.95 • Softcover • 304 pp. • ISBN 978-1-891824-40-1

**Shamanic Secrets Lost Wisdom REGAINED**

Shamans and Healers through Robert Shapiro Bring Back Lost Wisdom

## Shamanic Secrets: Lost Wisdom Regained
### Book D

Due to wars, natural disasters, a shaman not being able to train a successor, and many other reasons, Isis (through Robert) says that 95 percent of the accumulated shamanic wisdom has been lost. Now it is important to regain this wisdom as young people who are able to learn and use these processes are being born now.

Beings who lived as shamans and healers on Earth at various times now speak through Robert Shapiro and bring these lost teachings and techniques to a humanity waking up and discovering it has the talents and abilities to use this wisdom for the benefit of all.

$16.95 • Softcover • 352 pp. • ISBN 978-1-62233-049-2

## THROUGH DRUNVALO MELCHIZEDEK

# THE ANCIENT SECRET
# OF THE FLOWER OF LIFE,
## VOLUME 1

Once, all life in the universe knew the Flower of Life as the creation pattern, the geometrical design leading us into and out of physical existence. Then from a very high state of consciousness, we fell into darkness, the secret hidden for thousands of years, encoded in the cells of all life.

Now we are rising from the darkness, and a new dawn is streaming through the windows of perception. This book is one of those windows. Drunvalo Melchizedek presents in text and graphics the Flower of Life workshop, illuminating the mysteries of how we came to be.

Sacred geometry is the form beneath our being and points to a divine order in our reality. We can follow that order from the invisible atom to the infinite stars, finding ourselves at each step. The information here is one path, but between the lines and drawings lie the feminine gems of intuitive understanding.

$25^{00}$  Softcover, 240 PP.
ISBN 978-1-891824-17-3

You may see them sparkle around some of these provocative ideas:
- remembering our ancient past
- the secret of the Flower unfolds
- the darker side of our present/past
- the geometries of the human body
- the significance of shape and structure

Drunvalo Melchizedek's life experience reads like an encyclopedia of breakthroughs in human endeavor. He studied physics and art at the University of California, Berkeley, but he feels that his most important education came after college. In the past twenty-five years, he has studied with over seventy teachers from all belief systems and religious understandings. For some time now, he has been bringing his vision to the world through the Flower of Life program and the Mer-Ka-Ba meditation. This teaching encompasses every area of human understanding, explores the development of humankind from ancient civilizations to the present time, and offers clarity regarding the world's state of consciousness and what is needed for a smooth and easy transition into the twenty-first century. ℨ

## THROUGH DRUNVALO MELCHIZEDEK

# THE ANCIENT SECRET
# OF THE FLOWER OF LIFE,
## VOLUME 2

The sacred Flower of Life pattern, the primary geometric generator of all physical form, is explored in even more depth in this volume, the second half of the famed Flower of Life workshop. The proportions of the human body; the nuances of human consciousness; the sizes and distances of the stars, planets, and moons; and even the creations of humankind are all shown to reflect their origins in this beautiful and divine image. Through an intricate and detailed geometrical mapping, Drunvalo Melchizedek shows how the seemingly simple design of the Flower of Life contains the genesis of our entire third-dimensional existence.

From the pyramids and mysteries of Egypt to the new race of Indigo children, Drunvalo presents the sacred geometries of the reality and the subtle energies that shape our world. We are led through a divinely inspired labyrinth of science and stories, logic and coincidence, on a path of remembering where we come from and the wonder and magic of who we are.

Finally, for the first time in print, Drunvalo shares the instructions for the Mer-Ka-Ba meditation, step-by-step techniques for the re-creation of the energy field of the evolved human, which is the key to ascension and the next dimensional world. If done from love, this ancient process of breathing prana opens up for us a world of tantalizing possibility in this dimension, from protective powers to the healing of oneself, others, and even the planet.

Topics Include
- The Unfolding of the Third Informational System
- Whispers from Our Ancient Heritage
- Unveiling the Mer-Ka-Ba Meditation
- Using Your Mer-Ka-Ba
- Connecting to the Levels of Self
- Two Cosmic Experiments
- What We May Expect in the Forthcoming Dimensional Shift

**$25**$^{00}$ Softcover, 272 PP.
ISBN 978-1-891824-21-0

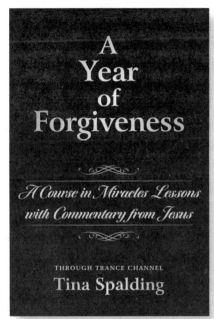